To our late and greatly missed mom, Cristeta, and dad, Felix Sr., who brought ten of us into this world, and raised us honorably despite their poverty,

To my darling children, Rhea, Liza, Reynaldo Jr., Melisande and Ana Angelica, for giving me five reasons to go on living,

To my wife, Ophelia, for standing by me through thick and thin,

To the Almighty God, for everything that I am and have,

I dedicate this little piece of work.

Acknowledgments

A book, even of this modest size and depth, cannot be possible without the ideas, material support and encouragement of colleagues and friends who, in varying degrees, contributed to its making.

I am specially indebted to:

Raul A. Mabini, a dear friend and fellow alumnus of the Asian Institute of Management, incumbent Baybay City budget officer and former vice-president for the Visayas of the Philippine Association for Government Budget Administration, Inc., for his material support and for encouraging me to pursue the publication of this book.

Liza, my daughter, for patiently doing the numerous layouts I required with each revision.

Mr. Eusebio M. Abenio, erstwhile managing director of Seed, Inc., for his invaluable technical inputs and for encouraging me to document my experiences into a process guide product.

Dr. Peter Hartig, former adviser to Seed, whose searing and thoughtful critiques led me to a series of revisions on the content of the Municipal Enterprise Development Plan of Boljoon, Province of Cebu;

Mr. Jaime S. Dechos, my closest colleague and partner at Seed, and Mr. Hubert Zanoria, who served as planning officer of the Philippine-German Cebu Upland Project (Cup), for their thoughtful technical inputs.

The Community Development Workers of Cup who served as masterful facilitators of the Barangay Strategic Planning Workshops in Boljoon.

And last, but not least, to all farmers; fisherfolk; women; out-of-school youth; Barangay Council persons; Sangguniang Bayan; Dr.

Rene E. Amper, then municipal mayor of the Municipality of Boljoon, Province of Cebu; and representatives of other social sectors in Boljoon without whose time, deep thoughts and active participation in the processes involved in the formulation of the Boljoon Municipal Enterprise Development Plan, this book would not have been written.

Author

Introduction

A landmark legislation, the Local Government Code (LGC) of 1991 brought about a radical change in Philippine governance. Ending a long era of centralized administration, the LGC literally empowered the local government units (provinces, cities, municipalities, barangays) to shape development according to their own terms. Through a process of decentralization, the LGUs were given more powers, authorities, responsibilities and resources, thereby enabling them to fully develop as self-reliant political units and as effective partners in the attainment of national goals. Pursuant to local autonomy, certain national government functions were devolved to the LGUs. These functions cut across such sectors as agriculture and fisheries, infrastructure, environment, social services and health.

Alongside the devolution of the foregoing responsibilities, the LGC decentralized certain national government powers and authorities. These include the powers to levy taxes, fees and charges; to equitably share in the proceeds from the exploitation of natural resources located within the LGU territories; to borrow from local and foreign sources; to engage in economic ventures; and to allocate resources in accordance with the plans, policies and programs formulated by special local bodies and ratified by the LGU legislative bodies. In addition, the Code raised the internal revenue allotments (IRA) of the LGUs and mandated their automatic releases.

Yet, more than two decades now since the passage of the LGC, local autonomy still remains a dream for a large number of LGUs. Far from growing into self-reliant and effective partners in the attainment of national goals, a good number are in fact faced with serious problems of coping with their devolved responsibilities. Indeed, while the Code devolved certain functions of the central government, it stopped short of devolving the budget necessary to meet the high costs of devolution. Even as the LGU IRAs have been rising substantially, these have not been enough to meet the costs of devolved personnel and services. Such is particularly true of the low-income LGUs, many of which remain too cash-strapped to even absorb the full salaries and benefits of devolved employees. No wonder, then, that there would be clamors from devolved municipal workers for re-nationalization.

It is obvious that policy reforms are imperative if local autonomy must happen across all LGUs. Some areas where reform is deemed necessary include: the iniquitous IRA distribution formula; ambiguous formula and mechanism for determining the sharing of proceeds from the utilization of national wealth located within the LGU territory; and planning, budgeting, and funds control for nationally funded programs and projects implemented by LGUs.

Beyond reforms in the foregoing areas, there is the need to look deeper into the social preparation of LGUs. For that matter, results of *Rapid Field Appraisals of Decentralization* conducted since 1992 by the Associates in Rural Development (ARD) for the USAID-funded **Governance and Local Democracy** (Gold) project reveal that, whether for lack of technical know-how, fear of political consequences or over-dependence on the IRA, the LGUs have been rather slow in using their revenue-raising powers and have performed poorly in local resource generation. The ARD noted that technical capability is virtually absent at the level of the barangay. These findings suggest that unless the LGUs learn the ropes of self-reliant governance, increases in IRA levels are not likely to make any meaningful impact on the lives of their poor constituents.

It was against this backdrop that the Small Economic Enterprise Development, Inc. (SEED) decided to embark on developing what is now the Municipal Enterprise Development Plan (MEDP) technology as a critical intervention in support to the local autonomy directions of the government. A local partner of the Friedrich Ebert Stiftung Foundation, SEED is a national business consultancy NGO with which the author was connected as senior consultant from January 1992 until July 1994. Through a six-month consultancy contract with the German Technical Cooperation Agency, SEED was commissioned to facilitate the formulation of the MEDP for the Municipality of Boljoon, Province of Cebu—for purposes of identifying what livelihood opportunities were feasible in light of the natural and human resource base of the area. Boljoon is one of three southern Cebu municipalities covered by the *Philippine-German Cebu Upland Project*, a bilateral undertaking of the Government of the Philippines and the Federal Republic of Germany.

The Boljoon experience paved the way for SEED to develop and launch the Local Enterprises Advancement Program for Local Government Units (LEAP-LGUs) sometime in 1993 or so. With the MEDP as a focal product line, the LEAP-LGUs used to be actively marketed by SEED and its network of small business institutes to local government units in the Visayas, Luzon and Mindanao regions and offered a menu of technical assistance services. After Boljoon, succeeding applications of the MEDP process that the author is aware of were made in Calbiga, Western Samar, Philippines; Compostela, also in Cebu Province, Philippines; Bingawan, Iloilo Province, Philippines; Carigara, Northern Leyte Province, Philippines; Biliran, Biliran Province, Philippines; Magalang, Pampanga Province, Philippines; Maydolong, Eastern Samar Province, Philippines; and Tabon-Tabon, NorthernLeyte[1]. In 2011, the author had the opportunity of leading a team that facilitated

---

[1]   The author served merely as resource person to the Tacloban-based Institute of Small Business, Inc. Which anchored the formulation of the Calbiga MEDP. He did not stay with Seed, Inc. Long enough to see through the drafting of the municipal enterprise development plans of the municipalities of Compostela and Bingawan.

the transfer of the planning technology to all barangay captains of Quezon City, Metro Manila, Philippines in collaboration with i-Learn, a Metro Manila-based training institute. The latter subsequently facilitated the same applied training for all chairs of the Sangguniang Kabataan of the city.

This book captures the *participatory* processes involved in the formulation of the MEDP. It is so written to serve as a handy guide to the formulation of a municipal enterprise development plan and, necessarily, the barangay enterprise development plans.

The MEDP is essentially a strategic economic masterplan. As such, it provides but a road map, as it were, to a municipality's or a city's journey to development. It is meant to serve principally as an initial step to rationalize local enterprise promotion and development as a long-term strategy to raise the revenues of LGUs, the low-income especially, thereby enabling them to meet the requirements of local autonomy. Truly, more than the government, the private sector is it that creates the bulk of employment opportunities for our people. With employment, income and savings are generated. And with savings, capital is formed and mobilized to expand the existing businesses or create new ones, in effect generating new jobs and income opportunities for the local people. If this cycle is sustained over a long time, imagine how the local economy can be able to absorb the incremental local labor force members every year. In the end, enterprise development broadens the tax base of the LGU, raising therefore its revenues without even having to raise the existing tax rates or without imposing new tax measures. And with higher revenues, the LGU becomes empowered to improve or expand the delivery of basic social services to its constituency, resulting in a contented, happy people.

The network analysis shown on Figure 1 illustrates just these cause and effect relationships.

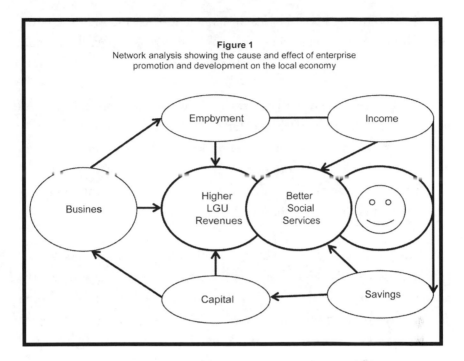

Figure 1
Network analysis showing the cause and effect of enterprise
promotion and development on the local economy

The author began writing this manual in 1995, clear about who its potential readers and, hopefully, users would be. And they include the following:

- The Municipal Mayors, City Mayors and Provincial Governors and their Planning and Development Staff because theirs is the delicate responsibility of planning and managing development at the local level;
- The local and national NGOs because they, too, are at the forefront of development management in their geographic areas of operation; and
- The universities and colleges because theirs is the crucial task of preparing the youth for eventual participation in nation-building, not only as development managers but even more as future leaders destined to inevitably take over the reins of government from their elders.

Although models of economic development plans abound, one hardly finds, if at all, a material that shows *how* to prepare one. This book, therefore, is an attempt to help fill this void.

On the other hand, without casting aspersion on our colleges and universities, how many of us graduate from such courses as economics, public administration, rural development, enterprise management, community development, or social work reasonably equipped with the tools necessary to be of help in the development of our communities? It is hoped that this applied manual can be of help in this direction.

There are institutions which technical publications and formal trainings provided the author a great deal of ideas that shaped the contents of this handbook. They include, among others, the *Asian Institute of Management* where the author took up two non-degree courses; the *Philippine Business for Social Progress* where he first trained in strategic planning and decision-making, and the *National Council for Integrated Area Development* which publications provided a wealth of ideas on the subject.

Reynaldo B. Almenario

Table of Contents

Chapter 1

Meaning of Development

"Sustainable development is development or progress that meets the needs of the present without compromising the ability of future generations to meet their own needs."

BRUNDLAND COMMISSION
OUR COMMON FUTURE

Introduction

Until today, development remains one term whose definition continues to stimulate intellectual debate the world over.

Economists equate development with economic growth, measured in terms of the country's gross national product (GNP), or the money value of all goods and services produced in a country over a certain period of time, usually a year. More than this, they hold that growth must be accompanied by or brought about by technological efficiency, that is to say, the ability of a country to increase output per unit of input.

Other economists go even farther. For that matter, *Kindleberger*[2] asserts that development (read: growth) also implies changes in the structure of outputs and in the allocation of inputs, by economic sector. It is not enough that the GNP grows. Development must also reflect changes in the contribution of certain sectors to overall output. An

---

[2]   Charles P. Kindleberger, ***Economic Development,*** 2nd Ed. (Evanston, Illinois: Northwestern University Press, 1988) p.3

increasing contribution of manufacturing to the GNP, for instance, implies that a country may well be on the way to an industrial status.

This concept of development became the basis for judging the performance of governments. Political success became simply a matter of raising the GNP, a measure of how wealthier the country has become.

GNP Drawbacks

As measure of a country's development status, the GNP has been criticized for its shortcomings. The GNP, say its critics, among whom Prof. Eduardo Morato, Jr. of the Asian Institute of Management is one of the most profound, leaves pretty much of development unaccounted for. It does not measure good health, nutrition, leisure, safety, happiness, ecological balance. Indeed, a good many productive activities of the citizens are left out in the GNP accounting: housekeeping by wives and family members; backyard gardening; preventive health care; breast-feeding of infants; mothers, fathers and other family members tutoring their school kids; nuns taking care of the sick, nurturing the spirits and minds of the young in school and begging for alms to give to the poor; community self-help projects that improve the environment for better living . . .*ad nauseam*.

On the other hand, the GNP incorporates such counter-productive, anti-development, even anti-life activities as production of weapons of mass destruction; wars; production of harmful chemicals and pesticides; investments in factories and automobiles that pollute the air, endanger the health of people and irreparably destroy the ozone layer; alcoholic beverages and cigarettes that shorten the life-span of drinkers and smokers; etc. Against the claim that the GNP per capita is a good measure of individual welfare, the critics say it is misleading as it assumes equal sharing of the national wealth, forgetting that there are capitalists and workers, feudal lords and *sacadas*, landlords and tenants, househelps and housemasters.

Truly, the increasing GNPs of nations from the days of Adam Smith do not necessarily mean richer people, even as they did bring and continue to bring enormous wealth to the very few. Then and now, empirical evidence has shown that there exists, even in the highly "*developed*" nations, a wide chasm between affluence and poverty, between the rich and the poor. The social inequalities, let alone the continuing damage on the global environment spawned by the liberal capitalist development model, would later move Karl Marx and Friedrich Engels to collaborate in the development of the communist ideology. Which espouses a classless society.

Outlandish as their dream of a utopian state may be, Marx and Engels contributed a great deal to the debate on the essence of *development*. Their attack on the excesses of liberal capitalism would pave the way to the emergence of more humane, pro-people development models espoused largely and more aggressively by non-government organizations (NGOs) and people's movements around the world, most particularly in the Third World in which the Philippines belongs.

Emerging Concepts

Today, well-meaning efforts at defining development as an end have brought to fore a host of profound concepts propounded by institutions and individuals in the thick of development work. Below are some thought-provoking propositions.

- Development is a basic human right and, therefore, it is for all people.
- Development is primarily for the disadvantaged, those who do not have enough of the basic necessities of a decent, human living.
- Development should look beyond mere creation of wealth to how wealth is distributed.

- Development is sustainable growth, one that meets the needs of the present without compromising the ability of future generations to meet their own needs.
- Development is one that ensures equity and promotes people's participation.
- Development, says Prof. Morato, is a community or societal effort (people first); it is collaborative, not competitive (people working for people); and it is concerned with the welfare of each and everyone (people fully actualizing themselves as people should). The GNP, as a yardstick of development, should exclude activities that impair the mind, body, spirit and the environment, and include instead new elements that value health because it provides a good life; nutrition because it enables people to work; education because it transforms character, molds the minds and builds skills; safety because it allows freedom of action and offers peace; leisure because it liberates the body and the mind; and happiness because it suffuses the spirit.

Synthesis

From the foregoing thoughts, we may then propose to define development in the following terms:

Development is *sustainable growth of all people, by all people and for all people.*

By this definition, development acquires a democratic character as it should, and implies the fundamental right of all people to enjoy the basic amenities that go with it. Understood in the context of a right, development becomes as much a responsibility or obligation of all people to make it happen. In addition, by this definition, the critical element of economic growth still comes into play. But we hold, rather strongly, that growth as such is meaningless, let alone scandalous, if the bulk of its benefits accrue only to the few of society, leaving the broad majority with hardly enough to keep body and soul together. By this logic, economic growth that stops short of sharing its benefits with all people—with the underprivileged most especially—cannot pass for genuine development. It is, at best, a prescription for social unrest. Such was the experience in France as it has been in Latin America; indeed, such was (and still is) our very own experience.

Moreover, we argue that development must be *sustainable*: one that happens never at the expense of the present and future generations. As such, development efforts must pay high premium on the management of the environment and its scarce resources, thereby ensuring the survival of the present and future generations.

Likewise, we believe that development must happen through people's participation (*by all people*). Prof. Morato distinguishes between two models of development according to their ability to involve the people. One is the turtle model and the other, the centipede model. With the first model, Morato likens the art of governance to a turtle that has a small head, four feet and a large body. The small head with its four feet symbolizes the leadership, trying to pull the large body (symbolizing the people) forward. With this model, the people hardly participate, if at all, in development. No wonder, then, that growth happens very slowly, that is to say, at turtle's pace.

In contrast, with the second model, Morato likens the art of *participatory* governance to a centipede. Its head symbolizes the political leadership and its numerous feet symbolize the people ambulating together to pull the body forward. This explains why the centipede moves faster than the turtle. With this model, then, development is expected to happen relatively faster because the people are actively involved in the various phases of building a nation, a region, province, city, municipality, or barangay. Truly, short of people's participation, development becomes virtually an act only by those who wield political and economic power, leaving the people merely as passive beneficiaries. This is no development. This is dependency.

Meanwhile, we also believe, as the economists argue, that economic growth must reflect technological advancement, enabling us to raise output per unit of input, in effect enabling us to produce at the least cost. In so doing, we improve our competitive position, improving therefore our chances to survive in this new millennium when *trade globalization* would have fully governed our economic life.

Somehow, we must graduate from being principally a producer of raw materials to being a raw materials processor. In this manner, we not only generate value-added that translates into new jobs and income opportunities for our people; we also prolong the shelf life of our products, in effect enabling our producers to stabilize their prices.

And that means we need *to develop our capacity to manufacture the means of production*, that is to say, the machines, engines and tools that can, for instance, turn our coconut meat into premium coconut oil, bio-diesel, coconut methyl ester, aflatoxin-free expeller cake and other products; and the coconut husk into coir fiber, geo-textile, coir dust, coco peat, granulated charcoal or charcoal briquette. The basic difference between an industrial country and a pre-industrial one, says Lichauco,[3] is the capacity of the former to manufacture the means of production, which the latter does not possess. It is this capacity that enables the former to create wealth to a limitless degree, which translates into its astounding capacity to create employment and income opportunities for its people. A look into the structure of the Philippine economy and other third world economies vis-à-vis such developed economies as the U.S.A. and Japan (see Table 1) would give us a glimpse of this basic difference.

---

[3]   Alejandro Lichauco, **Nationalist Economics**, (Makati, Metro Manila: Society of St. Paul, Inc., 1988), p. 270.

**Table 1. Comparative Share of Agriculture and Industry
in the Gross Domestic Product, by Country[4]**

(in percent)

COUNTRY INDUSTRY	AGRICULTURE	INDUSTRY
U.S.A.	2	32
Japan	3	41
Ethiopia	48	16
Central African Republic	39	20
Philippines	12	31

Observe, on the one hand, the nominal role of agriculture in the economies of the U.S.A. and Japan and the dominant role that industry plays, on the other. The reverse is true of such third world economies as Ethiopia and the Central African Republic, both of which are heavily dependent on agriculture. And while the Philippines appears to be more industrial than agricultural, a look into the country's sectoral contribution to total employment elicits a different picture, as depicted in Table 2.

Table 2. Sectoral Contribution to Total Employment, October 2011

SECTOR	EMPLOYMENT (IN PERCENT)
Services	52
Agriculture	15
Industry	33
Total	**100**

Source: National Statistics Office, Philippines.

---

[4]   Data for U.S.A, Japan, Ethiopia and Central African Republic are sourced from Lichauco's book, Na- tionalist Economics, p. 271-272, and refer to 1984. Philippine figures are sourced from the National Statistical Coordination Board and refer to 2012.

It is clear from the table above that agriculture is not only the poorest employer but also the smallest contributor to the country's gross domestic product (GDP). This means quite clearly that we remain trapped in our pre-industrial status—like Ethiopia and the Central African Republic of 1984.

The Philippine challenge, then, is to industrialize enough to be able to absorb its burgeoning labor force, and lift millions of our people from the sub-human conditions to which poverty, as a function of underdevelopment, has consigned them. And that means we have to begin manufacturing the means of production that creates wealth and multiplies labor a million-fold. Lichauco (op. cit.) argues that the inability of a people to produce the machines, engines and tools that enable them to multiply labor severely limits their capacity to generate the goods and services they need, in effect rendering their survival dependent on the industrial powers who exploit that dependence and perpetuate it.

The task is not at all impossible if only our policy makers and economic managers had serious concern for genuine industrialization, and respect and recognition for the ingenuity of our native inventors. Once upon a time, in the decade of the '50s, we were second only to Japan in terms economic development. But look where South Korea, China, India, Singapore, Malaysia, Taiwan, Indonesia and Thailand are now. Trailing us once before, many of these countries have become new "Japans," while the others—by choice—are fast entering into such a status.

No, this is not to say that we put agriculture behind us. Rather, let agriculture benefit from an industrial revolution by providing it the basic agricultural machines, engines and tools that multiply muscle-power while creating enormous employment and income opportunities for our people. In the final analysis, without an efficient agriculture sector providing the raw materials base, there can never be any meaningful industrialization to begin with.

Chapter 2

Development Process

Introduction

But how do we proceed to attain *development* as we defined earlier? The process of achieving sustainable growth of all people, by all people and for all people has been known as *development management*. And those whose task is to manage the development of a geographic area, be it a country, region, province, municipality, city or barangay, are called *development managers*.

As a formal discipline, development management is relatively a new field in the Philippines. A recognized pioneering institution in this regard is the Asian Institute of Management, which offers degree and non-degree courses and has in fact graduated a good many development managers from all over Asia.

Meanwhile, the practitioners are agreed that development management is a lot more complex than straightforward business management. Prof. Morato, an acknowledged guru, explains that while the business manager can simply focus on a singular objective as profits, the development manager, in contrast, must attend to diverse and, oftentimes, conflicting objectives, e.g., land distribution versus economies of scale; environmental protection versus investment promotion and development to create local jobs and income opportunities; participatory decision-making versus business management efficiency; and so forth and so on. This suggests that development management requires a host of expertise: a business manager quick at discerning and exploiting opportunities for profit; an economist knowledgeable in optimum allocation of scarce resources; an environmentalist with a good grasp of ecology; a political scientist skilled in the dynamics of decision-making and power; a sociologist adept at understanding how people live and interact with each other; and a lot more.

Of course, very few, if at all, would have all of the capabilities singled out above. And that is why the development manager must be able to identify and harness as much individual and institutional expertise critical to the development of his or her geographic area as there are. Therefore, the ability to identify and mobilize local and external resources is a key quality that a development manager ought to possess.

To go back to our question, how do we proceed to propel a geographic area as a municipality to sustainable growth?

To be honest about it, there is no sure formula or sure route to this dream. The reason is that there exists no local showcase of a municipality, barangay, city or province that has attained development as we defined in the previous chapter. Palawan may qualify as an excellent model for environmental management, but may be far off as an economic or political development showcase. In any case, let's be consoled in the thought that sustainable development is still a new paradigm, one that rose to global prominence only on occasion of the first Earth Summit held in Rio de Janeiro in 1992, where the subject was exhaustively deliberated as Local Agenda 21.

Even so, we are fortunate that there is Prof. Morato's work now embodied in his book, *Strategic Intervention for Development Managers*, that we can turn to as an interesting treatise on how a geographic area may be propelled to development. Briefly, Prof. Morato speaks of three wheels of the development vehicle: (1) the environmental wheel; (2) economic wheel; and (3) the socio-political wheel. The delicate task of the development manager, he says, is to propel balanced growth (read:

sustainable growth) while aboard these three wheels. Let us discuss these in turn.

The Environmental Development Process

According to Morato, environmental development, as indicated by a higher level of productivity and better quality of life, results from a process of optimizing the use of resources belonging to a geographic area, to an industry or sector, and to a development agency, with the latter becoming an effective catalyst in the process.

Industry or *sector* refers to enterprises and institutions with common or inter-related products or services. One example is the coconut industry and its participants that include farmers and their organizations; farm workers and their organizations (if any); traders and their organizations; processors and their organizations; and industrial workers and their organizations. Another is the livestock and poultry industry and its participants that include the growers and their organizations; farm workers and their organizations (if any); feed millers and their organizations; food processors and their organizations; industrial workers and their organizations; and the traders and their organizations and employees.

On the other hand, the *agency* can mean any government entity, business firm, NGO, people's organization or political party which is involved in the development of a geographic area.

There are three interfaces where the manager of a development agency can intervene, says Morato. One is the *area and agency interface* which calls for effective management by the agency of the area's resources for purposes of harnessing, utilizing and controlling these resources. This interface is necessarily supported by the creation of area or local administrative mechanisms. Some popular examples of the latter are the Laguna Lake Development Authority, Metro Manila Development Authority and the Subic Bay Development Authority.

Another is the *area and industry/sector interface*. This occurs at various levels ranging from the utilization of the area's resources (as land, labor, savings, natural resources, infrastructure, knowledge resources, etc.) to the conversion of these resources into investments (as capital, buildings, technologies, machinery and equipment, raw material, etc.) and the creation of backward (supply) and forward (market) linkages with other geographic and industrial/sectoral organizations. The best manifestation of this interface, according to Morato, is the creation of enterprises or institutions.

Finally, there is the *agency and industry/sector interface*. This involves the mobilization or build-up of industrial/sectoral capabilities and the promulgation of industry/sector incentives and regulations. This linkage is forged by the creation of industry/sector authorities and associations, as exemplified by such bodies as the Fiber Industry Development Authority, Philippine Coconut Authority, National Book Development Board, and the various associations of abaca and coconut farmers and publishers. Figure 2 depicts Morato's environmental development model.

The Economic Development Process

Economic development, as indicated by general prosperity and equity, results from a process of converting resources into investments; investments into goods and services; goods and services into income; and income plowed back into resources or distributed to the intended beneficiaries (see Fig. 3). To paraphrase Morato, the economic development process involves the four basic arithmetic operations of multiplication, addition, subtraction and division.

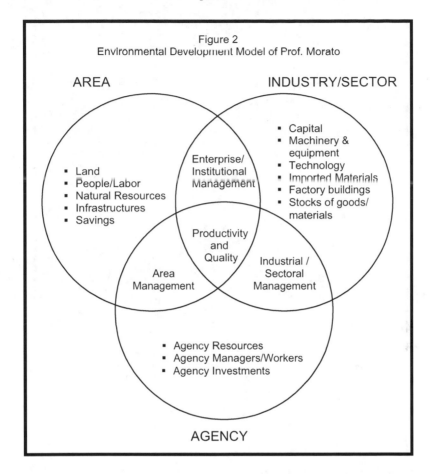

Figure 2
Environmental Development Model of Prof. Morato

AREA

INDUSTRY/SECTOR

- Land
- People/Labor
- Natural Resources
- Infrastructures
- Savings

Enterprise/
Institutional
Management

- Capital
- Machinery &
  equipment
- Technology
- Imported Materials
- Factory buildings
- Stocks of goods/
  materials

Productivity
and
Quality

Area
Management

Industrial /
Sectoral
Management

- Agency Resources
- Agency Managers/Workers
- Agency Investments

AGENCY

The multiplication process can occur in various ways. One is by processing the raw materials into various products, thereby multiplying employment and income opportunities. This process is best exemplified by the coconut industry which provides a number of raw materials that can be processed into various marketable products. The meat can be turned into virgin oil; oil into soap, bio-diesel and 2T oil; copra meal into animal feed; coconut husk into coir fiber, geo-textile, coco peat and other products; coconut shell into charcoal; coconut water into vinegar; and many more. Imagine the number of jobs created at each stage of processing the coconut raw material and its by-products.

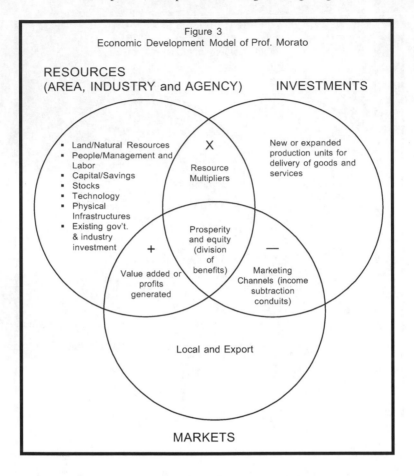

Figure 3
Economic Development Model of Prof. Morato

RESOURCES
(AREA, INDUSTRY and AGENCY)   INVESTMENTS

- Land/Natural Resources
- People/Management and Labor
- Capital/Savings
- Stocks
- Technology
- Physical Infrastructures
- Existing gov't. & industry investment

X
Resource Multipliers

New or expanded production units for delivery of goods and services

+

Prosperity and equity (division of benefits)

−

Value added or profits generated

Marketing Channels (income subtraction conduits)

Local and Export

MARKETS

Morato identifies three alternatives with high multiplier effects. One is to harness production inputs with nearly zero cost. These would include idle labor, idle or underutilized lands, or idle capital goods as machinery and equipment and factory buildings. Another is to leverage scarce resources, that is to say, using resources other than one's own. This is exemplified by an NGO that opens a guarantee fund with a bank for the benefit of its farmer-borrowers and is, in turn, granted a credit line many times bigger than the guarantee fund. In effect, this enables the NGO to serve the credit requirements of more farmers. And still another alternative is to focus on a critical input of production, marketing or finance rather than provide all inputs which will only put to bear on the capacity of the agency to deliver. A critical input can be an irrigation system serving the requirements of a large number of rice farms; a credit mechanism that liberates a large number of farming households from the clutches of usurious money-lenders; an advanced ratooning technology that reduces substantially the cost of producing palay while improving the yield; or a bridge that would cut transport/marketing cost considerably.

The addition process happens when the goods and services are sold to the market, revenues realized and values are added to the economy. The process presumes, of course, that revenues exceed costs; otherwise, no economic development occurs because there is neither growth in wealth nor is there extra income to distribute to the beneficiaries or to plow back to the resource base. As such, the addition process presumes the operation of viable enterprises.

Similarly, the subtraction process occurs when the goods or services are marketed to buyers and sellers. Traditionally, marketing has been participated in by intermediaries or distribution channels which collect commissions or profit margins, reducing therefore the potential income of the producers or manufacturers. The intermediaries, of course, perform a critical role in bringing the goods and services to the consumers. Without them who invest substantially in warehousing and trucking, let alone credit, much of the output turned out by producers and manufacturers would hardly reach the end or intermediate users.

Nevertheless, there are distribution channels that are better by-passed as a way to raise the prices received by the basic producers on the one hand, and reduce the prices paid by end-users, on the other. And one way to achieve this objective is to provide the producers with information on alternative markets, or enable them to perform certain functions played by marketing agents such as warehousing and trucking.

Finally, the division process involves the sharing of profits or value-added. Morato asserts that, without profit-sharing among those who took part in the process, no real development can ever occur. The more equitable the distribution of benefits is, says Morato, the more extensive the process of economic development becomes. This suggests that the cooperative system—in contrast to corporations, partnerships and single proprietorships—offers, theoretically, the best organizational alternative to achieving a more equitable distribution of benefits. Of course, this system, like any other, has its own drawbacks. Among others, the slow process of decision-making, general lack of business acumen, lack of transparency and the inability of most cooperatives to improve the lives of their members are some issues that presumably continue to deter a good many from joining the cooperative movement.

Be that as it may, there are cooperatives, no matter how few, that perform just as well, if not better than corporations, partnerships and single proprietorships. They are tangible testimonies that the cooperative system remains a viable proposition that need to be promoted extensively as it ensures equitable distribution of the windfalls of development among the participants.

The Socio-Political Development Process

Meanwhile, the weaknesses besetting most cooperatives in the country have something to do with individual and organizational inadequacies, whether behavioral, technical, financial or managerial. This brings us to Morato's last wheel of the development vehicle: the socio-political development process which aims at human infrastructure and institution-building. Socio-political development, explains Morato, is a social process because it is concerned with the development of healthy relationships of individuals within an organization and of groups inter-acting with other groups and the environment they live in. It is also a political process because it deals with empowering people. Both social and political dimensions involve the art and science of people management. Morato advises, therefore, that the socio-political development process encompass the totality of the human being: the mind, the body and the spirit. By the same token, the process must consider the totality of people's institutions: their ideology, their organizations and their values.

There are three interfaces in this process. These are the ideology and organization (or society) interface; ideology and values interface; and organization or society and values interface.

Ideology interfaces with the organization or society through education and training which develops the organization's capabilities and unifies the mind, body and spirit. This interface, says Morato, is an *abstraction process* in that the organization's vision, ideas, theories, doctrines and beliefs are abstracted into a comprehensive set of education and training program, processes and tools for mental assimilation by the organization, resulting in the unity of the mind, body and spirit.

On the other hand, the interface between organization and values is an *action process*; it is where the value systems of the organization are reinforced, in effect raising the willingness to act and achieve the organization's mission and vision. This implies that the prescribed organizational values must be shared by the people, or must reinforce what the people hold dear. For only then will they willingly act along organizational objectives.

Finally, the interface between values and ideology is a *reflection process*. This is where values are internalized by the mind inasmuch as these jibe with the ideology. Described by Morato as the marriage of the mind (read: ideology) and the spirit (read: values), this process leads the members of the organization or society to commit to the ideals of the organization. We see this marriage notably happening within the folds of the CPP-NPA and other underground rebel groups which have succeeded to win the minds, bodies and spirits of their members.

In sum, organizational maturity and unity are the objectives of the entire socio-political development process. It is one of raising the consciousness and the capacity of the organization or society to a level of maturity where it can stand on its own, strengthened by the power of a unified people. Morato has identified various entry points where the development agency can initially intervene in this process. At the people level, it can intervene in terms of advocating an ideology, organizing individuals into operative groups, riding on existing value systems and mores, or using a combination of two or all possible entry points. At the organization level, the agency may intervene by introducing an improved production technology, by assessing the business operations of the organizations, by facilitating a strategic planning exercise, by identifying and analyzing training needs, or by using a combination of two or all possible entry points. In any case, the modes of intervention would be shaped necessarily by the agency's development agenda and its resources.

Figure 4 depicts Morato's socio-political development model.

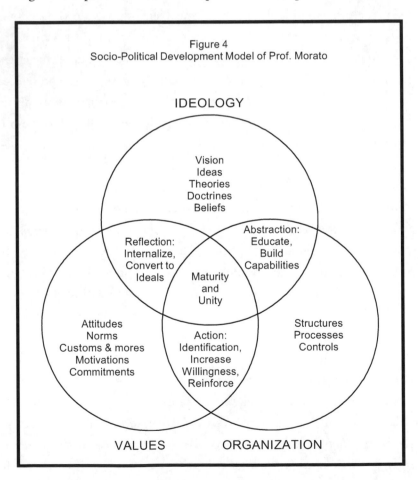

Figure 4
Socio-Political Development Model of Prof. Morato

IDEOLOGY

Vision
Ideas
Theories
Doctrines
Beliefs

Reflection:
Internalize,
Convert to
Ideals

Abstraction:
Educate,
Build
Capabilities

Maturity
and
Unity

Attitudes
Norms
Customs & mores
Motivations
Commitments

Action:
Identification,
Increase
Willingness,
Reinforce

Structures
Processes
Controls

VALUES   ORGANIZATION

Chapter 3

Organizing the Planning Team

Introduction

D evelopment planning cannot be carried out by a lone planner, no matter how versatile she or he may be. Perhaps, the most serious shortcoming of a good number of development plans in the hands of the LGUs is that, by and large, these are principally products of a lone mind. In most cases, economic planning rests on the Municipal Planning and Development Coordinator (MPDC) who is often the only guy manning a think-tank that the Municipal Planning and Development Office (MPDO) is supposed to be. In some municipalities, the MPDC doubles as Civil Registrar or as head of the Business Permit Section.

Given this situation, it becomes easy to understand why a good many of existing development plans with the LGUs reflect quite clearly the bias of the lone planner, a bias necessarily influenced by his or her discipline and work experience. Thus, an engineer-MPDC is most likely to produce an infrastructure-heavy development plan just as the agriculturist planner is likely to turn out an agriculture-heavy document.

Team Composition

What is a fairly good planning team composed of? The answer is, "It depends." It depends on the development area's available resources, both natural and human, that the LGU wants to convert into attractive investments. It is important, therefore, that the LGU executives possess a good grasp of the potentials of their barangays, municipality, city or province. This knowledge allows the planning team to zero in on the key development areas.

Even if the LGU decides to engage the services of an external consultant, this knowledge is still imperative. For, in the absence of that knowledge, it becomes difficult to draft the Terms of Reference (TOR) relative to the consultancy engagement. Among other things, the TOR, which is an important document that goes with the consultancy contract, spells out clearly the objectives of the LGU and defines the output it expects from the consultant. Without the TOR, the consulting organization will find it difficult to staff the planning team.

To go back to the question, what is a fairly good enterprise development planning team composed of? A typical composition is presented in Table 3.

Table 3. A Typical Composition of an MEDP Planning Team

POST	QUALIFICATION	TASK
Team Leader	Graduate of Economics, Business Administration, Rural Development, Community Development and related disciplines.	Serve as chief facilitator of planning workshops.
	With hands-on knowledge and experience in strategic planning.	Lead the planning team in all processes involved in MEDP formulation.
	Strong in technical writing.	Provide coordination and supervision over the planning team.
Crops Specialist	Graduate of Agriculture, major in Agronomy.	Anchor the assessment of the status of major agricultural crops raised in the development area, including its potentials for other high-value crops.
	At least 3-year experience as agronomist.	Anchor the identification of crops-based enterprises.

POST	QUALIFICATION	TASK
	Basic know-how in natural resource management.	Assess the efficiencies of technologies in use.
	Can write acceptable reports.	Collaborate with Market Analyst in assessing the existing production of major crops vis-à-vis consumption requirements.
		Recommend measures to improve productivity and enhance local capacities in appropriate technologies. Provide estimates of investment requirements for selected crops-based enterprises.
Livestock Specialist	Graduate of Agriculture, major in animals.	Anchor the assessment of the status of major animals raised in the development area, including its potentials for the production of other animals.
Livestock Specialist	At least 3-year experience as animal scientist.	Assess the efficiencies of technologies in use.
	Can write acceptable reports.	Collaborate with Market Analyst in assessing the production of major animals vis-à-vis consumption requirements.
		Anchor the identification of animal-based enterprises.
		Recommend measures to improve productivity and enhance local capacities in appropriate livestock raising technologies.
		Provide estimates of investment requirements for selected animal-based enterprises.
Sociologist	Graduate of Sociology.	Assess the characteristics and trends of the local population and labor force.
	Know-how in making population projections.	Anchor the identification of trade and other skills locally available.
	Can write acceptable reports.	Project the local population over the next 5-10 years.
Civil Engineer	Graduate of Civil Engineering.	Anchor the assessment of the status of infrastructure facilities.
	At least 3-year experience in planning and implementing civil works projects.	Anchor the identification of infrastructure critical to the promotion and development of local enterprises.

POST	QUALIFICATION	TASK
	Can write acceptable reports.	Provide cost estimates for upgrading existing infrastructure facilities and the construction of new ones.
		Anchor the production of necessary maps.
Fisheries Specialist	Graduate of Fisheries.	Anchor the assessment of the coastal and freshwater resources in the development area.
	At least 3-year experience in planning and implementing coastal resource and/or freshwater management projects.	Collaborate with Market Analyst in assessing the productive capacity of the area's coastal and freshwater resources vis-à-vis consumption requirements.
	Can write acceptable reports.	Anchor the identification of fisheries-based enterprises.
		Anchor the estimation of investment requirements for fisheries-based enterprises.
		Recommend appropriate measures to rehabilitate and protect the area's coastal and freshwater resources.
Market Analyst	Graduate of Marketing, Economics and related courses.	Anchor the assessment of markets for the products of selected livelihood projects.
	Applied knowledge of statistical projection tools.	Collaborate with Fisheries Specialist, Crops Specialist and Animal Specialist in assessing the local agricultural and fisheries production vis-à-vis consumption requirements.
	At least 3-year experience in marketing or socio-economic research and analysis.	
Institutional Development Specialist	Can write acceptable reports. Graduate of Management and related courses.	Anchor the conduct of internal analysis and assessment of the institutional environment.
	At least 3-year experience in planning and managing institution-building and human resource development programs.	Recommend appropriate interventions necessary to develop local capacities in various areas critical to local enterprise promotion and development.
	Can write acceptable reports.	Provide estimates of costs associated with capacity building.

There can be more or less to the foregoing composition, depending upon, as we said earlier, the types of resources and the priorities of the LGU. If there are significant metallic or non-metallic mineral deposits in the area that the LGU wants to harness, for instance, then obviously there is a need to engage the services of a metallurgist or a mining engineer to assess their development potentials.

Sourcing the Planning Team Members

Most of the skills singled out above can be sourced within the municipal government workforce. Table 4 below suggests where the planning team

Table 4. Where to Source the Planning Team members

POST	POSSIBLE SOURCE	
	Main Source	Alternative Source
Team Leader	Municipal Planning & Development Office	Externally hired
Crops Specialist	Office of the Municipal Agriculturist	Office of Provincial Agriculturist
Livestock Specialist	Office of the Municipal Agriculturist	Office of Provincial Agriculturist
Fisheries Specialist	Office of the Municipal Agriculturist	Regional Office, Bureau of Fisheries
Sociologist	Municipal Planning & Development Office	Externally hired
Civil Engineer	Municipal Engineer's Office	Provincial Engineer's Office
Market Analyst		Externally hired
Institutional Development Specialist	Office of the Municipal Agriculturist	Externally hired

For a municipality just beginning to do serious economic planning, the Team Leader (TL) is probably the most difficult to locate locally. Ideally, TL should be the Municipal Planning and Development

Coordinator. But should the latter's economic planning skills fall short of the requirements of the job, the LGU can engage the short term services of an experienced economic planner—only to transfer the necessary planning technology, particularly to the Municipal Planning and Development Office. In this regard, there are alternative consulting institutions that interested LGUs can reach. These include the Tacloban-based Institute of Small Business, Inc. which has assisted a number of LGUs in Region 8 in the formulation of municipal and barangay enterprise development plans; Seed, Inc. and its network of small business institutes, which pioneered in the preparation of municipal enterprise development plans in the country; and the Metro Manila-based Management and Allied Services Specialist, Inc. of which the author is president.

Chapter 4

The Planning Process

"Plans are nothing; planning is everything."

DWIGHT D. EISENHOWER

The Need to Plan Development

D evelopment does not happen by chance. It begins with a *vision of the desired future*, and a vision necessarily shared by the people, for only then would they be compelled to rally behind it.

Yet, vision alone, no matter how inspiring and compelling, does not lead to development. The vision must be translated into a *plan*. The former defines the goal; the latter shows the way that leads thereto. Without a plan, we become like the mariner without a map or compass, unable to steer the boat to the right port of call.

Of course, the country's local government units (LGUs) are no strangers to development plans. Periodically, each municipality, city, or province formulates its own plan upon which budgeting is based. By and large, these plans are strong in infrastructure projects, on the one hand, but weak in livelihood development, on the other. Such imbalance is reflected in the budgets of a good number of LGUs, which allocate the largest portion of their development funds to infrastructure, indicating quite clearly the level of priority accorded to livelihood creation vis-à-vis infrastructure development.

Provision of support infrastructures is certainly critical to economic development. But without a clear-cut development plan to support in the first place, a pro-infrastructure budgeting practice can create, at best, only momentary employment and income opportunities for the local population. We like to believe that this common weakness is generally rooted in the technical inadequacy of LGUs to prepare a serious development plan, not to mention their incapacity to pay for the high cost of consultancy services.

Planning Framework

A widely used framework in both micro and macro planning involves four basic questions, as follows:

1. What does the environment permit us to do?
2. What do we want to do?
3. What can be done?
4. What should be done?

The first question seeks information on the opportunities to exploit and the threats to avoid in the environment, including the strengths and weaknesses of the LGU as an organization. Kotler,[5] an internationally noted marketing expert, defines *opportunity* as *"as an attractive arena for relevant marketing action in which a particular company is likely to enjoy a differential advantage."* On the other hand, he defines *threat* as *"a challenge posed by an unfavorable trend or specific disturbance in the environment that would lead, in the absence of purposeful marketing action, to the stagnation or demise of a company."*

For purposes of area development planning, let us define *opportunity* as *"an attractive arena for relevant production and marketing action in which a particular barangay, municipality, city or the province as a whole*

---

[5]   Philip Kotler, *Marketing Management: Analysis, Planning, Implementation and Control,* 2nd Ed. (Tokyo: McGraw-Hill Book Company, Inc.; 1965) p.99-100.

has a competitive advantage relative to other producing areas." And let us define *threat* as *"a challenge posed by an unfavorable trend or specific disturbance in the environment which would lead, in the absence of a purposeful social and political action, to the stagnation or retrogression of the local economy."*

The second question seeks information on the *values* of the LGU as a development agency, including the various social sectors which have stakes in the development of the barangay, municipality, or city. Values find expression in the vision, mission, goals, objectives and priorities of the LGU, line agencies of government, NGOs, funding agencies, and people's organizations operating in the development area. Likewise, values find expression in the people's religious, cultural and political beliefs. Information on values is critical to generating a profile of livelihood preferences, by barangay and by social sector.

The third question seeks to determine what opportunities are feasible in light of the opportunities and threats in the external environment; the strengths and weaknesses of the LGU; and the values of the various development actors.

Finally, the fourth question involves the drafting of the enterprise development plan that embodies the key stakeholders'[6] decisions on what development vision to pursue, what mission should the LGU assume relative to the vision, what objectives to set and what strategies to implement by way of attaining the objectives and, eventually, the vision.

---

[6]   Key stakeholders include, among others, the LGUs (municipality, city, province, and barangay), POs, NGOs, development agencies of government operating in the area, colleges and universities.

The Process

The foregoing framework shapes the processes involved in the formulation of the municipal or city enterprise development plan.

To respond to the question, "**What does the environment permit us to do?**," we perform two types of environmental analysis: *external analysis* and *internal or organizational analysis.* The first seeks to identify the opportunities and threats in the external environment; and the second the strengths and weaknesses of the LGU as an organization.

To the question, "**What do we want to do?**," we perform *value analysis*, the output of which is a profile of livelihood preferences of various social sectors in the development area.

To the question, "**What can be done?**," we perform the *matching process* to generate a profile of feasible opportunities.

Finally, to respond to the question, "**What should be done?**", we formulate the *Barangay Enterprise Development Plan (BEDP)* which embodies the decisions of each social sector on:

- what enterprises to promote and develop;
- why these should be promoted and developed;
- when these ought to be set up;
- how much it would cost to set these up; and
- what support services and facilities are necessary to raise their chances for survival, stability and growth.

Figure 5 captures the processes involved in the formulation of the municipal or city enterprise development plan. Detailed discussions of each process are treated in Chapters 5-9.

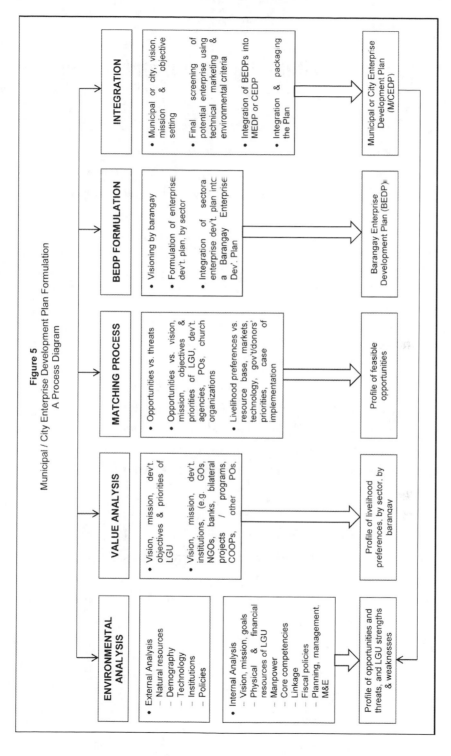

Figure 5
Municipal / City Enterprise Development Plan Formulation
A Process Diagram

Chapter 5

How to Facilitate Environmental Analysis

*"In the context of world economic growth, sustainable development has
a vital role to play in reminding businessmen that their business strategy
should always incorporate environmental protection as a major principle."*

Y. A. M. Tunku Naquiyaddin Ibni Tuankaja'afar
Chairman
ANTAH HOLDINGS BERHAD

Objective

Environmental scanning and analysis is done to search for answers to the question, *"What does the environment permit us to do?"* This exercise seeks to identify the *livelihood opportunities* in the external environment, the *threats to avoid*, and the *strengths* and *weaknesses* of the LGU (i.e., municipal government and the barangay) as a development agency.

To this end, we perform two types of analysis: (1) *external analysis* to draw out the opportunities and threats in the external environment; and (2) *internal or organizational analysis* to identify the strengths and weaknesses of the LGU (i.e., municipal government and the Barangay Council) as development agency.

External Analysis

In this exercise, we look into the various elements of the *external* environment. For purposes of municipal enterprise development planning, the following environmental elements are relevant.

▪ *Natural Resource Environment*

This environment provides the life-blood of development. Always the starting point in any economic development process, this element covers all the natural resources present in the development area. The components of this environment may include all of the following:

- land area;
- forest products;
- fresh water resources;
- crops;
- animals and fowls;
- minerals;
- climate and rainfall;
- fishing grounds;
- coastal resources;and
- potential tourist spots.

Characterize these resources according to their size; their uses (i.e., products produced); the possible future uses that these can still be put into; their present status/conditions/problems and their causes and effects; their ownership structures; their current levels of development; the constraints to their full development; and their present and potential capacity to support the consumption requirements of the local population.

Analysis of this environmental element should be able to identify the more promising resources based on such criteria as magnitude or size of the resource; significance of the resource with respect to the socio-economic life of the people; and the products that can be derived from the resource under existing technologies, including their market potentials.

A checklist of information on the natural resource environment is presented in Exhibit 1.

Exhibit 1

Data Checklist: Natural Resource Environment

I.   **Soils and Climate**

    A.   To what type of climate does the barangay belong?

    B.   What is the average monthly and annual rainfall?

    C.   Is there a distinct dry or wet season? Which months are dry and which are wet?

    D.   Is the barangay located within the typhoon belt? During which months is typhoon expected?

    E.   What types of soils are present in the barangay? Which type is most dominant? What is status of the barangay soils? What have brought this about? What crops are suitable?

II.   **Land Area and Land Use**

    A.   What is the total land area (in hectares) of the barangay?

    B.   How much of the total area is devoted to:

        1.   Agriculture?

        2.   Forestry?

        3.   Human settlements?

        4.   Industrial and commercial centers?

        5.   Institutional uses? (e.g., schools, chapels, barangay hall, barangay basketball/tennis court, market building, etc.)

    C.   How much of the total land area is idle?

    D.   What are the major agricultural crops in the barangay?

        1.   How much area is devoted to each crop? What is the average yield of each crop per ha?

        2.   How many families are dependent on each crop for livelihood?

        3.   How is the production of each crop disposed of? How much (in percent) goes to:

            3.1 markets?

3.2 *home consumption?*

3.3 *seeds/planting materials?*

3.4 *animal feeds?*

3.5 *others? (specify)*

4. Where are the major crops of the barangay traded?

5. In what forms is each major crop traded?

    5.1 *raw?*

    5.2 *if processed or semi processed, in what forms?*

6. What is the prevailing price received by farmers for each major crop in each market during:

    6.1 *harvest time? (specify months)*

    6.2 *lean months? (specify months)*

7. What are the problems/issues confronting each major crop? What are the causes? What have been the tangible effects? What have been done by whom regarding these problems/ issues? What are the results?

8. What other uses can each major crop be put into?

9. What is the dominant tenurial arrangement prevailing for each major crop? How many families are land-owners? owner-cultivators? share tenants? lessees or CARP beneficiaries?

10. What is the annual average income of farm household, by major crop raised?

11. What are the major animals (livestock/poultry) being raised in the *barangay*?

12. What is the current population per animal?

13. What are the current uses per animal? How much (in percent) of the production of each animal goes to markets? home consumption? used as work/draft animal?

14. In what forms is each animal traded by the *barangay*?

15. How much of the output of each animal (in percent) is traded live? as meat?

16. What is the prevailing price received by farmers for each type of animal?

17. What problems/issues confront the production of each animal? What are the causes? What have been done by whom regarding these problems or issues? What have been the results?

E. How big is the forestland of the *barangay*?

    1. What tree species are thriving?

    2. How big is the area (in hectare) covered by each tree specie?

3. Is there any reforestation program being implemented in the *barangay*? Who undertakes the program? How much area (in hectares) is covered? Who finances the program? What is the present status of the program?

4. What are the problems/issues confronting the forestland of the *barangay*? What are the causes? What have been done by whom regarding these problems or issues? What have been the tangible effects of these problems?

5. How many families depend on forest products gathering?

   5.1 What forest products are gathered?

   5.2 In what forms are these traded?

   5.3 Where are these traded? at what prices?

III. **Fisheries/Coastal Resources**

A. How large (*in hectares*) is the fishing ground of the *barangay*?

B. How many families are principally dependent on fishing?

C. What is the daily average fish catch (in kilos) per fisherman during:

   1. abundant months? (*specify months*)

   2. lean months? (*specify months*)

D. How is the daily fish catch disposed of? How much (*in kilos*) goes to:

   1. markets?

   2. home consumption?

E. Where is the fish catch of the barangay traded?

   1. What is the prevailing price (*per kilo or any local unit of measure*) received by fishermen per type of marine product?

   2. What is the average daily fish catch per operator during:

      2.1. abundant months?

      2.2. lean months?

   3. Where do the commercial fishing operators dispose of their fish catch?

F. In one year, how many months are devoted to fishing activity?

   1. What do the fishing families do for a living during periods when fishing is not possible?

G. What problems/issues confront the fishing sector in the barangay?

   1. What are the causes?

   2. What have been the tangible effects of these problems?

   3. What have been done by whom regarding these issues? what have been the results?

H. Are there fishponds in the *barangay*?

1. What is the total *fishpond* area?

2. How many operators are there?

3. What marine products are produced?

4. How much (kilos) is produced, by type of marine product?

5. In what forms are these traded?

    5.1 Where are these traded?

    5.2 At what prices?

IV.   Minerals

A. What minerals are found in the *barangay*?

B. How much deposits (*in metric tons*) are there per type of mineral?

C. What extraction activities are being done? by whom?

    1. What minerals are extracted?

    2. How much is extracted per year?

    3. Where are these sold? at what prices?

D. What problems/issues confront the mineral resources in the barangay?

    1. What are the causes?

    2. What have been the tangible effects?

    3. What have been done by whom regarding these problems? What have been the results?

▪ *Technological Environment*

Technology, says Kotler, is the most dramatic force shaping human destiny.[7] If natural resources provide the life-blood of development, technology provides the engine that has brought humanity to amazing heights of progress.

We, therefore, scan the technological environment to take stock of the technologies currently adopted in the locality, including those clearly relevant to the development of the natural and human resources locally available.

---

[7]   Ibid., p. 112-114.

The review of this environment will cover technologies in such economic sectors as agriculture and fisheries; trade and industry; and services. The assessment is expected to generate information on the productive capacities of existing technologies; their product or service quality characteristics; their unit costs; and their impact on the environment. In addition, this assessment may identify and locate technologies superior to those in use in the locality, including technologies critical to the production of new products or services derivable from existing resources. A partial data checklist for use in assessing the technological environment is provided in Exhibit 2.

Exhibit 2
Data Checklist: Technological Environment

I.   **<u>Agriculture</u>**

  A. **Crops**

      1.   How does the average yield of each major crop in the barangay compare with yields attainable under existing technology recommended by the Department of Agriculture (DA)?

      2.   How does the average cost of producing each major crop compare with the cost under the DA-recommended technology?

      3.   How does the quality of each major product of the barangay compare with those produced in other areas in terms of size, texture and other quality features considered by buyers?

      4.   How does the buying price of each major product of the barangay compare with those of similar products produced by other areas and traded in the same markets tapped by the barangay?

      5.   In what forms is each major crop of the barangay traded?

          5.1 raw?

          5.2 processed? in what specific forms?

      6.   What other products can be derived from each major crop under existing technologies available with the Department of Science and Technology or with other technological institutions?

      7.   How does the dominant technology used in the production of each major crop affect the environment?

          7.1 fosters soil erosion?

          7.2 denudes the forests?

          7.3 reduces soil fertility?

7.4 pollutes the rivers and seas?

7.5 conserves, rehabilitates and protects the environment? etc.

8.   What agencies have been extending technological know-how to the barangay? What services do these agencies offer? What have been the results of their interventions?

9.   Does the present output of each food crop meet the consumption requirements of the barangay today and in the years to come?

B.   Animals

1.   What is the dominant scale of producing livestock and poultry in the barangay? Backyard? Commercial?

2.   What types of animal stock are available to animal raisers in the barangay? High-breed? Native? Cross breed?

3.   Where do they obtain their stock? At what prices?

4.   What types of animal feeds are predominantly used by raisers? Commercial? Local formulations? Kitchen left-overs?

5.   What agencies have been extending technological know-how to the animal raisers in the barangay? What services or assistance have been extended to the barangay? What have been the results?

6.   How much does it cost to produce each unit of animal? How does this compare with the average cost of production under the technology recommended by the DA?

7.   What stands in the way to the commercial production of animals in the barangay?

8.   Does the present production of livestock and poultry meet the protein requirements of the barangay today and in the years to come?

II.   **Fisheries**

A.   What is the most dominant system of producing marine products in the barangay?

B.   How much does it cost to produce per unit (i.e., kilo) of output, by production system?

C.   What production systems are considered harmful to the coastal environment? How do these adversely affect the environment? How many fishers are into these practices?
     What have been done by the authorities, environment-oriented NGOs, if any, and the people in this regard? Does the existing production meet the consumption requirements of the barangay today and in the years to come?

1.   What is the monthly production capacity of each?

2.   How many workers does each producer employ?

3.   What principal raw materials are used, by type of product? Where are these sourced? At what prices?

4.   What is the producer's price, by type of product?

5.   How much does it cost to produce each product?

D.   Who are the principal buyers, by type of product? Where are they located?

E.   What problems (e.g., technology, finance, marketing, management, skills availability, etc.) are faced by the producers of these products?

F.   Does the production of each product adversely affect the environment of the barangay or other areas? If so, how?

▪ *Demographic Environment*

People make up the most crucial element in the environment. With our ingenuities, we not only make development happen for us, or against us, we also make up markets. Such is why the first environmental element of interest to the business person is population.

In scanning and assessing the demographic environment, we look into the characteristics and trends of the population in our barangay and our municipality. In particular, we look into the following:

Total population;
Geographic distribution;
Population density;
Number of families and average family size;
Number of households and average household size;
Population by sex;
Population by age group;
Population by income class;
Population by occupational group;
Annual growth rate;
Income and expenditure patterns;
Average household income and expenditure;
Poverty incidence and poverty sectors;
Educational levels;
Ethnic/cultural groups;
Religions;
Birth and death rates;

Leading causes of morbidity and mortality;

Migration patterns;

Labor force and employment/unemployment; and

Skills.

Likewise, we look at the population of neighboring municipalities and cities which are potential markets for the surplus production of the development area.

A data checklist for assessing this environment is provided in Exhibit 3.

Exhibit 3
Data Checklist: Demographic Environment

I.   **Total Population**

A.   What is the latest population count in the barangay?

B.   How many families presently compose the barangay?

C.   How many households are there at present?

II.   **Population Characteristics**

A.   How is the current population distributed according to:

    1.   sex?

    2.   age group?

    3.   occupation? (e.g., farming, fishing, business, employed professionals, farm labor services, other services, etc.)

    4.   religion?

    5.   Educational levels?

    6.   Ethnic origin?

B.   What are the birth and mortality rates?

C.   What are the ten leading causes of deaths and morbidity? D. Income and expenditures pattern.

    1.   What are the main sources of income of the people?

    2.   What is the average annual family income from all sources?

    3.   How much does the average family spend annually on the following basic items?

    3.1 food

3.2 housing

3.3 clothing

3.4 medicines, hospitalization

3.5 light

3.6 water

3.7 fuel

3.8 recreations

3.9 education

3.10 transportation

3.11 special occasions (e.g., fiesta, birthdays, Christmas, new year, death anniversaries, debuts)

4. What is the average family savings?

E. Labor force

1. How many compose the labor force of the barangay (i.e., 15 years old and over)?

2. How many are employed? unemployed? under-employed?

3. What are the principal sources of employment in the barangay? how many are employed in agriculture, fishery, trade and commerce, industry, services?

F. Population growth and migration

What is the average growth rate of the barangay over 1990-1998?

How many residents out-migrate to other areas every year? where do they go to? for what reasons?

How many people in-migrate to the barangay every year?

G. Trade skills/special talents

1. What skills are available in the barangay? (e.g., metalworking, carpentry, masonry, plumbing, beauticians, barbers, motorcycle driving, four-wheel vehicle drivers, auto mechanics, motorcycle mechanics, handicrafts-making, fine arts, music, etc.)

2. How many residents possess each of the foregoing skills/talents?

3. Are these skills presently utilized in the barangay for livelihood purposes?

H. Poverty incidence and poverty sectors

1. How many households earn below the poverty line?

2. What social sectors are particularly affected by poverty?

▪ *Institutional Environment*

This environment encompasses all development institutions external to the LGU, whether actual or potential intervenors in the development of the municipality. These would include: provincial government; line agencies of government; NGOs; local cooperatives; government and private banks; colleges, universities, trade and vocational schools; etc.

The foregoing are actual or potential sources of expertise, technologies, services and funds critical to the development of our municipality. Analysis of this environment will cover the mandates of these institutions, their target beneficiary groups, their existing services, programs and projects, including their plans during the next five or ten years.

Scanning and analysis of this environment is expected to generate information on external resources (e.g., financial, material, expertise) which can be mobilized to support the implementation of the enterprise development plan.

Exhibit 4 provides a checklist of information on this environment.

Exhibit 4
Data Checklist: Institutional Environment

A. What development institutions/agencies, whether government or non-government are currently operating in the municipality?

B. What is the mandate of each institution/agency, its vision, mission, and objectives?

C. Who are the target groups of each institution/agency?

D. What forms of assistance does each offer its beneficiary groups (e.g., technology, financing, technical/behavioral trainings, marketing assistance, etc.)?

E. What are the priority barangays, if any, of each institution/agency?

F. What are the existing programs/projects of each institution/agency?

   1. What is the nature of each project/program? Where is this located?

   2. How many families benefit from each project/program and in what ways?

3.   What is the total cost of each program/project?

F.   How many personnel does each institution/agency deploy in the municipality?

G.   What types of technical expertise does each institution/agency possess?

H.   What plans does each institution/agency have during the next five or ten years?

I.   What are strengths and weaknesses of each institution/agency in terms of manpower, skills, finances and management/organization?

J.   How does the public perceive each of this institution?

K.   What other institutions, whether private or governmental, whose presence the barangay people want? What services do they offer?

▪ *Policy Environment*

Finally, this environment encompasses all official laws, regulations, executive orders and investment programs at the provincial and national levels which either enhance or constrain the exploitation of certain natural resources, and the promotion and development of local enterprises. A partial listing of policy areas for review would include the following:

- Business taxation policies of the provincial and national governments;
- Agrarian reform law; GATT;
- Provincial and national investment priorities plans; Mining Act of 1995;
- Forestry and fishery laws;
- Magna Carta for Small and Medium Enterprises;
- Lending programs of LBP, Quedancor, Small Business Corporation, TLRC, and other government financing institutions;
- Agriculture and Fisheries Modernization Act;
- Local Government Code of 1991;
- Technical Education and Skills Development Act of 994;
- Customs duties;
- Buying policies of the National Food Authority; and
- Act creating the Cooperative Development Authority.

Assessment of this environment is expected to generate information, among others, on support programs and services currently available to local enterprises, including information on enterprises falling within the priorities of existing governmental development policies and programs.

Internal Analysis

Internal or organizational analysis looks into the following areas:

> Mandate of the development agency (municipal government and the Barangay Council);
> vision and mission (if any);
> Development priorities and plan;
> Financial resources and financial position; other physical assets as infrastructures; human resource and core competencies; resource allocation;
> Program/project monitoring and evaluation systems;
> Policies affecting local businesses and exploitation of local resources; and
> Linkages with external organizations.

This review is expected to identify the strengths and the weaknesses of the LGU as development agency. While information on strengths will be crucial to the making of choices as to which opportunities to exploit, knowledge of weaknesses will be useful in making *realistic* choices (see Exhibit 5 for checklist of information to use in assessing the local infrastructure resources and Exhibit 6 for checklist to use in local policies review).

Exhibit 5

Data Checklist for Assessing Local Infrastructure Resources

I. <u>**Road Network and Accessibility of the Barangay**</u>

A. What roads give access to the barangay?

B. What is/are the length(s) of this/these roads?

C. What is the status of these road(s)? Is/are this/these passable by all types of vehicle any day of the year?

D. What transportation facilities to and out of the barangay are available? What is the frequency of trips?

E. What are the transport costs (passenger and cargo), by type of transport facility?

F. Does the existing road network effectively link the local producers/business people to the local or external markets?

G. What road network needs to be put in place to give the producers better access to the markets? How much would it cost to construct this?

H. Does the local government have any plan to improve the existing road network or to open a new one? If so, what is the time-table?

II. <u>**Water Supply**</u>

A. What is/are the source(s) of portable water in the barangay?

B. How is the water distributed to the barangay households? By householdconnection? Communal faucet? Spring box? etc.?

C. What is the water supply situation? Adequate all year round? Inadequate?

D. What other economic uses are the existing water supply resources put into?

E. Is there an irrigation system in the barangay? If so, how many hectares are served?

F. What problems confront the water supply in the barangay? What are the causes? What have been done by whom regarding these problems? What have been the results?

III. <u>**Power Supply**</u>

A. Is the barangay electrically lit?

B. If so, how many of the households are served?

C. What economic activities have sprouted because of the presence of electricity? What existing economic activities are based on the availability of electrical power?

D. Who supplies electricity to the barangay? at what price/kilowatt hour?

E. If the barangay is not yet served by electricity, has the Barangay Council done anything to bring electrical service to the locality?

IV. <u>**Communication System**</u>

A. What are the means of communications in the barangay? Radio Stations? Post Office? Wire agencies? Etc.? Where are these located?

B. What is the most common means of communications used by the baranggay residents when in need of market information?

Exhibit 6

Data Checklist for Assessing the Local Policy Environment

I. **Local Business Taxation**

   A. What business taxes are imposed by the local government unit (i.e., Barangay Council, Municipal/City/Provincial Government)? What are the tax rates?

   B. How has the local business community reacted to these impositions?

   C. What tax incentives, if any, does the local and the national governments presently offer or plan to offer? What types of business are eligible?

   D. Does the local government unit intend to raise existing tax rates in the near future? If so, by how much?

   E. What new business taxes are planned to be imposed by the local government? What is/are the projected rate(s)?

II. **Business Registration and Business Permits**

   A. What procedures are prescribed by the local government in registering business entities and in securing business permits?

     1 How long does it take to register a business or secure a business permit?

     2 Can the process be shortened?

   B. How much does it cost to register a business or secure a business permit?

   C. What percentage of the total number of establishments in each barangay is registered or operates under a business permit?

III. **Government Regulations Relative to the Exploitation of Natural Resources**

   A. What natural resources in the locality are open to exploitation?

   B. What are the regulations relative to the exploitation of each resource?

   Which agencies of government regulate the exploitation of each resource? What are these regulations?

Sources of Environmental Data

The data used in the analysis of the various elements of the external and internal environment are generated from alternative sources. A listing of these sources, by type of information, is shown on Exhibit 7.

Exhibit 7
Alternative Data Sources, by Environmental Element

Element	Data Source
External Environment	
Natural resource environment	Key barangay informants MPDC Municipal Agricultural Office
Technological environment	Key barangay informants Municipal Agricultural Office Department of Trade and Industry Department of Science and Technology Technical Education & Skills Authority Agricultural colleges / universities Trade and vocational schools Bureau of Agricultural Statistics
Demographic environment	National Statistics Office Rural Health Unit MPDC Key barangay informants
Infrastructure environment	Municipal Engineer MPDC, Key barangay informants
Institutional environment	Key officers of the line agencies of Gov't., NGOs, POs, government and private banks MPDC Municipal Mayor Key barangay informants
Policy environment	BIR Provincial Treasurer's Office DENR DA, DAR, DTI Land Bank, DBP
Internal Environment	
Vision, mission, objectives, priorities and plan	Municipal Development Plan Municipal Mayor Key LGU informants
Financial resources and other assets	Treasurer Municipal Accountant Budget Officer Municipal Engineer Municipal Assessor
Manpower and core competencies	Mayor's Office Key informants
Linkages	Mayor's Office Office of the Municipal Agriculturist Office of the Municipal Engineer Office of the DSWD Officer MPDC
Program/project monitoring & evaluation systems	Mayor's Office, MPDC
Fiscal policies	Mayor's Office MPDC Treasurer's Office

Barangay Planning Workshops

By and large, planning data at the *barangay* level across the country are hardly available from secondary sources. To generate the bulk of information critical to the formulation of the municipal enterprise development plan, we organize two-day *barangay* enterprise development planning workshops. More than the generation of planning data, this activity provides an important venue for the active participation of all social sectors in the *barangay* from data generation and analysis to the drafting of the *barangay* enterprise development plan (BEDP). The participants, process and content of this workshop are discussed below.

Participants

To ensure that the MEDP embodies the aspirations of all social sectors, the planning workshop is designed such that a multi-sectoral participation is drawn. A typical composition of participants in this workshop is presented in Table 5.

If there are sectoral organizations in the *barangay*, it is wise that the workshop participants be sought from their ranks. In this manner, the resulting BEDP will have been more responsive to the needs and wants of each sector. Judging from the author's experience in Boljoon and Calbiga, the presence of the municipal mayor, at least in the opening ceremonies, is always fruitful. More than lending prestige to the exercise, the mayor creates the impression that the municipal government is serious about improving the lives of the people.

Meanwhile, to save on time and costs, it is wise that the planning workshops are conducted by cluster, of at most three *barangays* per cluster. Clustering may be made on the basis of the proximity of the *barangays* and the comparability of their economies.

Table 5. A Typical Composition of Barangay Planning Workshops Participants

SECTOR	NUMBER OF DELEGATES
Farmers	2
Fisherfolk	2
Women	4
Business	2
Out-of-School Youth	2
Barangay Council	2
TOTAL	14

Process and Content

A sample workshop programme is shown on Exhibit 8.

Exhibit 8
A Typical Programme for Barangay Strategic Planning Workshop

Day 1

7:30-8:00 a.m.	Arrival, checking in and registration
8:00-8:30 a.m.	Self-introduction of facilitators and participants
8:30-8:45 a.m.	Opening Remarks by Municipal Mayor
8:45-9:00 a.m.	Overview of the Workshop by Main Facilitator
9:00-9:15 a.m.	Merienda Break
9:15-9:20 a.m.	Introduction to 1st Exercise (by Facilitator)
9:20-12:00 noon	Exercise No. 1: External Analysis
12:00 noon	LUNCH BREAK
1:30-2:10 p.m.	Continue Exercise No. 1
2:10-3:10 p.m.	Group Output Presentation
3:10-3:40 p.m.	Open Forum
3:40-3:55 p.m.	Merienda Break
3:55-4:00 p.m.	Introduction to Exercise No. 2
4:00-5:00 p.m.	Exercise No. 2: Visioning
5:00-6:00 p.m.	Group Output Presentation
6:00-6:30 p.m.	Open Forum

7:00–8:00 p.m.	SUPPER
8:00–10:00 p.m.	SOCIALS
10:00 p.m.	CURFEW
Day 2	
8:00–8:05 a.m.	Ice Breakers by Participants
8:05–8:15 a.m.	Recap of previous day's sessions by Main Facilitator
8:15–9:15 a.m.	Technical Input: Defining a Business, Setting Objectives and Formulating Strategies (by Facilitator)
9:15–9:30 a.m.	Merienda
9:30–9:40 a.m.	Introduction to Exercise No. 3
9:40–12:00 noon	Exercise No. 3: Sectoral Project Planning
12:00 Noon	LUNCH BREAK
1:00–1:40 p.m.	Continue Workshop No. 3
1:40–4:40 p.m.	Enterprise Development Plan Presentation, by barangay
4:40–5:00 p.m.	Synthesis by Main Facilitator
5:00–5:15 p.m.	Distribution of Certificates of Attendance to participants

After the usual getting-to-know you portion and after establishing the rationale, objectives, methodology and outputs expected of the planning workshops, the participants go through the following exercises:

Exercise # 1: Environmental Scanning and Analysis

Briefly introduce the rationale of the workshop. Thereafter, break the participants into groups, by barangay, and make them select a discussion leader, a documentor and a presentor or presentors.

Then, ask all groups to do the following activities:

1. List all natural resources present in your barangay, including the skills available. Characterize these resources according to size or magnitude, present uses, possible future uses, present condition, status, problems and their causes.

2. From your list of natural resources, select at most five (5) resources that you consider most promising based on such criteria as size/ magnitude, market potentials and significance to the current livelihood of the people.

3. Characterize your LGU (your municipal or city government and your barangay) according to such factors as: budget; infrastructures; expertise in planning, monitoring and evaluation; resource allocation; linkages; and policy formulation and enforcement. What are its strengths? What are its weaknesses?

4. Identify the development organizations or institutions present in your barangay. Write down each in a separate metacard and paste the metacard inside a big circle drawn on a manila paper. Also identify the organizations or institutions not yet present in your barangay but whose services your barangay is in need. Write down each in a separate metacard and paste this outside of the big circle on the manila paper.

To enable a clearer picture of the outputs required, provide each group a sample accomplished output for each activity (see Exhibits 9-12). In addition, assign one facilitator to each group to provide clarifications when necessary and, most of all, to stimulate the active participation of the group members in the discussions.

Ask all groups to copy their final outputs into manila papers, using pentel pens. Thereafter, call a plenary for purposes of presenting the group outputs. The presentation creates an opportunity for the planning team to draw out more information on the barangay. Likewise, it is an opportunity to mutually deepen the team's and the participant's understanding of socio-economic realities and the development potentials of each barangay.

Expected Output

This exercise should be able to identify, to some extent, the livelihood opportunities open to each barangay, including the environmental threats it faces.

Time Requirement

For a cluster of three barangays, this first workshop requires at least six (6) hours: 4 hours to generate the information; one half hour to copy the outputs into manila papers; and 1.5 hours to present the outputs, including the open forum.

Required Materials, Supplies and Equipment

The following are needed for this process:

Manila papers;
Pentel pens;
Scotch or paper tapes;
Ball pens;
Yellow pad papers and bond papers;
Transparencies and transparency pens
(if electricity is available in the area);
Metacards;
Blackboard and chalk or whiteboard and whiteboard markers;
Overhead projector, if available and practicable.

Exhibit 9
Sample Output Format for Activity 1

Name of Barangay and Municipality _____
Province _____

Name of Resource	Size/ Magnitude	Unit	Present Status/ Problem	Causes	Present Use	Future Use
Total Land Area	600	Ha.				
Coconut	150	Ha.	Low production	Aging coconut tree Traditional Varieties	Copra, Charcoal, Coco, Lumber	Soap-making Nata de coco, Furniture
Palay	100	-do-	Low production	Low cropping intensity; No irrigation	Rice for home consumption	
Corn	50	-do-	Low production	Eroded soils; Lack of technology for upland farming	Corn Grains	Stalks as feed for cattle
Bamboo	50	Hill	Tight supply	Rampant gathering; No efforts at propagation	Housing materials King	Bamboo furniture
Fishing Grounds	600	Ha.	Low fish catch	Rampant illegal fishing	Fish catch sold raw by fishermen	Processed fish products

Note: All natural and human resources (i.e., skills) have to be inventoried and characterized

Exhibit 10
Sample Output for Activity 2

Name of Barangay and Municipality _____
Province _____

Most Promising Resource	Size/Magnitude	Unit	Dependent Families	Target Product	Potential Market
Natural					
Mango Plantation	10	Hectare	50	Mango Chips, Mango Juice	Supermarket, Groceries, Exporters
Cattle	200	Heads	100	Beef Fatteners	Households, Market Vendors
Native Chicken	2000	Birds	200	Live Birds	Barbecue Stall Operators
Human					
Basket Makers	10	Number	10	Bamboo Baskets	Farm Households, Other Households

Exhibit 11
Sample Format for Activity 3
Internal or Organizational Analysis

STRENGTHS		WEAKNESSES	
Municipal Gov't	**Barangay Council**	**Municipal Gov't**	**Barangay Council**
No debts	No debts	Low financial resources	Low financial resources
Dev't oriented chief executive	Supportive council	Poor road network	Poor access road
Committed manpower	Good relationship with mayor	Low technical expertise	Low technical expertise
Good relationship with governor and congressman		Resource allocation based on partisan politics	No linkages w/dev't agencies
Good linkages with development organizations, both government and private			Lack of political will to enforce ordinances

Exhibit 12
Sample Output for Activity No. 4

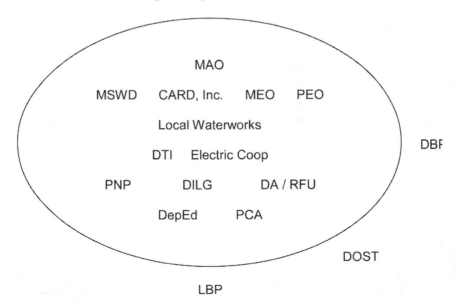

Chapter 6

How to Facilitate Value Analysis

"The genuine project derives its beginnings from the life of the people. It is a reflection of their values, their dreams and hopes, their joys, anxieties and fears. Anyone not in intimate touch with this life can, at best, produce counterfeit projects beneficial only to actors external to the rural poor."[8]

Objective

As we said earlier, value analysis is carried out to provide answers to the question, **"What do we want to do?"** Values in this sense refer simply to the livelihood opportunities the various social sectors in the barangay want to exploit as a matter of survival. Briefly, value analysis is expected to identify the core values of the participants, draw up a vision of each barangay, and define the mission (read: business) of each social sector relative to the vision.

Process

Three workshop exercises are facilitated to achieve the objective of value analysis. The first, labeled below as Exercise 2 to continue our sequencing from the first exercise, seeks to identify what the core values of the participants are; the second, labeled as Exercise 3, seeks to draw up a collective vision of the future they desire for their barangays and their

---

[8]   Ibid., p. 89.

people; and the third (labeled as Exercise 4) seeks to define their sectoral missions.

Exercise # 2: Core Values Identification

Core values are long-standing beliefs, aspirations, practices or customs that a society, community or organization holds dearly. They shape how people and organizations behave and act. They are what keep a society, community or organization together. Core values are the givens that a development manager must be aware of, respect and reinforce as he or she goes about developing and implementing strategies towards sustainable growth; otherwise, he or she is likely to meet resistance rather than acceptance and collaboration. Some examples are: education for children; good health; leisure; respect for elders; religiosity; united family; peace and order; decent, human living.

To draw out the core values, break the participants again into groups, *by barangay*. Give out 3 metacards to each participant. Then, ask the participants to respond to the following question:

> *As much as possible, in one to three words at most and in your dialect, name at most 3 things that you believe in or love most. Avoid arguments. Write each value on a separate metacard.*

After 10 minutes, ask the groups to consolidate the values into a group output, combine the similarities, and paste the cards on manila paper. Advise the groups to post their outputs on the board.

Thereafter, call a plenary. Clarify the group values to make sure that there is collective understanding and acceptance. Make the necessary changes as called for.

Exercise # 3: Vision-Setting

Vision is a picture of the desired future that a person, organization, sector, community or society wants to create. A good vision, according to visioning gurus as Scott, Jaffe and Tobe, is one that motivates, inspires commitment to action, clear, simple, realistic and reflects the core values of the person, organization, sector, community or society.[9] It is one that gives you goose pimples just by reading it.

Visioning is admittedly a difficult task. Scott et al describe it quite aptly as *"a journey from the known to the unknown, which helps to create the future from the montage of facts, hopes, dreams, dangers* (read: threats) *and opportunities."*[10] Difficult as it may be, visioning is an exercise always worthwhile. Our world is replete with stories of how success has gone largely, if not solely, to organizations and individuals driven by a clear image of the desired future. Necessarily rooted in current realities, the vision inspires commitment and action. Such is why visions need be crafted collectively, and communicated to the larger community so that these become a *shared* commitment and, therefore, a powerful force driving the community to the desired social or organizational transformation. There are alternative tools that we can use to facilitate vision-setting. These include imagery, story-telling and symbols.

Imagery is a process of taking the mind to a time in the future when the vision has been attained. What is our *barangay* like in this future? What are we like in this future? Having collectively visualized the future, it is translated into words, clear enough and persuasive enough to command community or organizational commitment and action.

---

[9]   Cynthia D. Scott et al, *Organizational Vision, Values and Mission,* (Menlo Park, California: Crisp Publications, Inc., 1993), p. 88.

[10] Ibid.

Story telling is a process of enacting the future, allowing the key stakeholders to experience the dialogue, actions and behaviors necessary to make the vision real. A play depicting what the *barangay* and its people would be like when the vision materializes can be created and acted out. The vision portrayed can then be captured into a clear, persuasive statement.

Finally, *symbols* are pictures, images or drawings that describe the vision. These are not necessarily artistic pictures or drawings. What is important is that these represent essentially the future desired by the stakeholders. Judging from the author's personal experience, use of symbols appears to be one very effective tool that makes the vision-setting exercise most memorable and enjoyable.

Visioning *gurus* advise that vision statements should be expressed in the present tense. Scott et al argue that expressing these in the future tense reinforces the gap between the present and the future; whereas expressing the future state in the present tense forces the question of how to emerge, with the creative tension that puts the vision into action.[11]

AFTER a 10-minute technical input on the concept and characteristics of a good vision, break the participants again into groups, *by barangay*, and ask them to do the following:

> *In your own dialect or in symbols (drawing), describe what you want to become of your barangay, as a place to live in, and as a people 10-20 years from now. Write or draw your vision on manila paper.*

Make available to the barangay groups all information that will facilitate the task of drafting their barangay visions such as results of

---

[11]   Ibid., p. 89.

environmental analysis (i.e., opportunities and threats, strengths and weaknesses) in which their visions should be rooted, and the core values that their visions ought to reflect. Moreover, make available some model visions, whether in statements or in drawings.

Exhibit 13 presents the vision statement of the Municipality of Calbiga, Samar. Note in particular the core values of the LGU that are apparent in this vision statement.

Exhibit 13
Vision Statement of the Municipality of Calbiga, Samar, Philippines

"By 2012, Calbiga is a livable and prosperous community, where people lead a decent, human living within an ecologically balanced, protected and safe environment. It serves as the center of trade and commerce for Western Samar and a well-known ecotourism destination in Eastern Visayas, in particular, and the Philippines, in general.

This sustainable progress is made possible by an empowered LGU and citizenry, believing in development as a right as much as it is a responsibility, able to discern what they are up to, what they are up against, where they want to go and how they want to get there."[12]

After 60 minutes, call a plenary and ask the barangay groups to present their barangay visions. Allow each group 5 minutes to make the presentation. Ask for clarifications as appropriate.

---

[12]   Adapted with some revision from the **Comprehensive Development and Land Use Plan** of the Municipality of Calbiga, Samar Province.

Keep the visions posted after the presentations as their owners would need to refer to these in the succeeding exercises. Likewise, the municipal planning team would later use these as relevant inputs to drafting the overall vision of the municipality. But be sure that, after use, these are returned to their rightful owners—the barangays—so that these serve the purposes for which they were crafted: as overall direction, as inspiration, as a compelling force towards social transformation.

Exercise # 4: Mission-Setting

Start with a 20-minute input on the concept of mission. In this regard, we define *mission* in the simplest way that Josiah Go in his book, *Contemporary Marketing Strategy in the Philippine Setting (1992),* defines it: *business.* The entertainer's business, for instance, is to make people happy; the priest's is to save souls; and the doctor's is to save lives.

The mission must be congruent with the vision, which is what the mission is meant to realize or attain. Go reinforces this idea when he argues that the purpose of business (read: mission) is the fulfillment of one's vision.

The mission needs to be articulated in a way that crystallizes its function, and provides the framework for developing objectives and strategy, for defining critical success factors, and for making resource allocation choices. The mission statement, say Scott et al (op. cit.), should evoke feeling and passion, and a personal response.

Exhibit 14 below reproduces the mission statement of the Municipality of Calbiga.

Now, look back to the LGU's vision statement in Exh. 12 and observe the apparent congruence and relationship between the mission and vision. Accomplishing the mission directly contributes to realizing the vision.

Exhibit 14
Mission Statement of the Municipality of Calbiga, Samar[13]

The Municipal Government of Calbiga is committed to:

Create local employment and income opportunities in close partnership with the private sector;

Formulate local policies supportive of the development of the micro, cottage and small enterprises (MCSEs) sector as well as the ecotourism sector;

Improve local capacities in sustainable utilization and management of natural resources, thereby securing the survival of the present and future generations of Calbiganons; and

Develop a professional and happy core of civil servants with a deep sense of public service."

Meanwhile, defining the business or mission of a profit enterprise is characteristically more direct and specific. In his book, Go offers some examples (see Exh. 15) of how company businesses or missions are defined based on their products or services.

---

[13] Ibid.

Exhibit 15
Some Examples of Mission or Business Definition[14]

PRODUCT OR SERVICE	BUSINESS OR MISSION
Railroad	Transportation or Moving people and cargo
Greeting cards	Personal expression
Auto repair	Providing safety drive
Photocopier	Office productivity
Telephone	Communication
Books	Knowledge

Quoting the 1960 manifesto, *Marketing Myopia*, of Harvard Professor Teodore Levitt, Go advises that the mission or business definition must be broad enough to allow the business "to expand, determine future products or to change faster in response to emerging opportunities or impending threats."[15] The *transportation* business, for instance, can go into products as trucks, cars, and airplanes just as the *office productivity* business can expand into such products as computers, facsimile machines and other similar items. Go shares the classic case of the railroad business in the United States which, according to Prof. Levitt, collapsed not because the need was provided by trucks, cars, airplanes and others but because it was not filled by the railroads themselves. On the other hand, Go cautions that too broad a business definition may defeat the purpose of defining what business we are in the first place.

AFTER the technical input, group the participants *according to the sectors* they represent in their barangays. Then ask them to do the following:

---

[14]   Joshiah Go, op. cit., p. 42.
[15]   Ibid., p. 41.

> *From the opportunities you have identified, select at most 5 businesses or missions that you would like to engage in so that you can contribute to realizing your barangay vision. Write these down on manila papers according to the prescribed format.*

Make available to each sectoral group, by *barangay*, a copy of the sectoral opportunities and threats they identified in Exercise 1 (i.e., Environmental Scanning) as well as the *barangay* vision they crafted. Also provide a copy of the prescribed format, according to which the output is to be presented (see Exh. 16 for sample). Assign one facilitator to each *barangay* group to help.

After half an hour, call a plenary and ask the *barangay* groups to present their outputs, by sector. Give each sectoral group 5 minutes to present. Allow the other groups to react. Be sure to subject each presentation to scrutiny so that the businesses are defined aptly.

The *Barangay* Council or the Local Government sector will necessarily have a mission statement different from the other sectors'. Expected to support and enhance the growth of local enterprises and not compete with them, this sector's business may involve, among others, the *development of support infrastructure* as *barangay* roads and bridges, irrigation system, electricity, trading infrastructure, and water system; *formulation and enforcement of support policies* such as the passage and enforcement of ordinance banning and penalizing owners of astray animals; *rehabilitation and protection of the barangay's natural resources* such as mangrove rehabilitation and enforcement of existing forestry and fishery laws; and the development of local capacities in natural resource management. Exhibit 16 presents a sample mission statement for this sector.

Exhibit 16
Sample Livelihood Preferences

Sector   Women
Barangay   Ciabu
Municipality & Province   Baybay, Leyte

RESOURCE	PREFERRED BUSINESS	PRODUCT
Coconut crop	Integrated coconut processing	Coco vinegar Coco charcoal Charcoal briquette Bio-diesel Coco peat Coir fiber Geo-textile Coconut oil
Banana	Food processing	Banana chips Banana cue
Cassava	Food processing	Cassava cake Cassava flour
Bamboo	Construction materials	Bamboo poles Bamboo splits
Ticog	Handicrafts making	Sleeping mats Placemats

Exhibit 17
Sample Mission Statement for the Local Government Sector

We commit:

To exhaust all means to upgrade or secure the support infrastructure facilities critical to the development of our community;

To protect and rehabilitate our forests, rivers, coastal and other natural resources so that these could adequately support the survival not only of our present but also our future generations; and

To develop local capacity in natural resource management and livelihood development.

Time Requirement

For a cluster of 3 *barangays* with 6 social sectors each, value analysis would require at most 240 minutes or 4 hours to accomplish: 20 minutes technical inputs; 20 minutes for core values identification; 60 minutes for visioning; 30 minutes for missioning; 95 minutes for presentations; and 15 minutes for synthesis.

Required Materials, Supplies and Equipment

Prepare the following for this process:

Summary of findings from environmental scanning and analysis;
Summary of opportunities and threats, and strengths and weakness of the barangay councils;
Vision and mission statements of the LGU, if any;
Overhead projector, if any;
Transparencies and transparency pens;
Manila papers;
Scotch or paper tapes; Meta cards;
Yellow pad, bond papers and ball pens;
Blackboard and chalk or whiteboard and whiteboard markers;
Sound system, if any; and
Computer and printer, if any.

Chapter 7

How to Facilitate the Matching Process

Objective

The matching process, as we said in Chapter 4, is carried out for one reason: to identify what *livelihood opportunities* are *feasible*. For purposes of municipal enterprise development planning, we use *feasible* simply in the context of livelihood preferences that possess *promising potentials* for survival and growth on the basis of certain pre-feasibility criteria.

The Process

Matching is a process of appraising the *apparent feasibility* of the livelihood preferences that surfaced in Exercise 4 (Chapter 6, Value Analysis) against such criteria as:

> local resource base;
> markets;
> technology;
> government and donors' priorities; ease of implementation; and
> employment generation capacity.

This is, by no means, a comprehensive set of criteria to govern enterprise selection. In any case, our objective is simply to share a system tried elsewhere, and hope this will stimulate the development of alternative systems more rational and more widely applicable.

TO START the process, make a recap of the preceding exercise with focus on its outputs. Then introduce Exercise # 5 as a sequel of Exercise #4. Explain what the exercise is meant to accomplish. Thereafter, break the participants into groups again, by *barangay* and by sector, and ask them to do the following:

Exercise # 5: Matching Process

> *In a scale of 1 to 5, rate the businesses you prefer against such criteria as: local resource base; markets; technology; government and donors' priorities; ease of implementation; and employment generation capacity.*

To facilitate this exercise, provide clues by posing the guide questions, by criterion, shown on Exhibit 18. A *positive* answer to each question necessarily calls for a rating of 3 and above.

Exhibit 18
Guide Questions for Matching Process

CRITERION	CLUE
1 Local resource base	➢ Can your local resources sustain the business? ➢ Are these resources renewable?
2 Markets	➢ Are there sure and stable markets for your products? ➢ Are product prices attractive and usually stable?
3 Technology	➢ Do you have local knowledge and skills required to produce the products? ➢ Will the business preserve and not destroy the environment?
4 Government & donors' priorities	➢ Does the business fall within the priorities of the national government and the local or international donor community?
5 Ease of implementation	➢ Can the business be made operational in the immediate term (less than 1 year)?
6 Employment generation capacity	➢ Will the business generate more than one job?

Enterprise Rating Form

The preferred enterprises are rated, by criterion, using the form shown on Exhibit 19 below. Rate the enterprise according to each criterion from 1 to 5. A rating of 1 connotes *Very Low*; 2 *Low*; 3 *Acceptable*; 4 *High*; and 5 *Very High*. Add the ratings and put the total on the space provided. Then, divide the total by 6 to arrive at the average rating for the enterprise and write this on the space provided. Finally, depending upon the average rating figure, characterize the enterprise into any of the following: Very High=average of 5; High=average of 4-4.99; Acceptable=average of 3-3.99; Low=average of 2-2.99; and Very Low=average of 1-1.99.

Exhibit 19

Sample Enterprise Rating Form

Enterprise Name:
Sector:
Name of Barangay:

	CRITERION	RATING
1	Local resource base	3
2	Markets	4
3	Technology	3
4	Government and donors' priorities	5
5	Ease of implementation	4
6	Employment generation capacity	3
	Total	22
	Average Rating (Total ÷ 6)	3.7
	Remarks	Acceptable

Legends for Average Ratings:
1 to 1.99= Very low;　2 to 2.99= Low　　3 to 3.99= Acceptable
4 to 4.99= High　　5= Very High

After 30 minutes, convene a plenary and ask the sectoral groups, by barangay, to present the outputs (written on manila papers) for purposes of comments and revision, if necessary. Post the final outputs on the blackboard or wall as these will be used as inputs in the succeeding exercise.

Time Requirement

This process takes at most 120 minutes: 10 minutes for technical input; 30 minutes for rating; and 80 minutes for output presentation critiquing.

Required Materials, Supplies and Equipment

This process requires the following materials and equipment:

Outputs of Exercise #4 on manila papers;
Guide questions to matching (shown on Exh. 17) written on the blackboard or on manila paper posted on the wall;
Enterprise rating forms (shown on Exh. 18);
Manila papers;
Pentel pens;
Scotch or paper tapes;
Ball pens;
Yellow pad papers or bond papers;
Transparencies and transparency pens (if electricity is available in the area);
Blackboard or whiteboard;
Chalk or whiteboard markers; and
Overhead projector pens (if electricity is available in the area).

Chapter 8

Barangay Enterprise Development Plan Formulation

Objective

This process responds to the planning question, **"What should be done?"** By the end of this process, the participants would have formulated their sectoral enterprise development plans, which are consolidated to form into the Barangay Enterprise Development Plan (BEDP).

Process

Begin with a recap of the immediately preceding exercise, with emphasis on its output. Emphasize that, to successfully carry out a mission or business, it is always wise to have a plan that would serve as guide to those implementing it so that they do not get lost on the way.

To facilitate this exercise, give a 60-minute technical input on the components of the BEDP, with emphasis on how to set SMART (i.e., specific, measurable, attainable, realistic, time-bound) objectives; formulate strategies to attain the objectives; prepare an implementation plan to set the strategies into motion; and prepare the corresponding budget to finance the implementation of the preferred business. Reinforce this input by showing *sample SMART objectives, strategies,* as well as *sample implementation* and *financial plan* (see Exh. 20-21 for samples). By experience, this has proved to facilitate the exercise.

Two types of objective are set: (1) development objectives; and (2) business objectives. The first is set around key result areas (KRAs) which may include: household income; employment; capacity-building; support policies formulation and enforcement; environmental rehabilitation and protection; accessibility; and the like. The second is set around such KRAs as: sales, market share, and profit.

Exercise # 6:
Sectoral Enterprise Development Plan Formulation

After the technical input, break the participants again into sectoral groups, by barangay, and ask them to do Exercise #6 and copy their outputs (in their own dialect) on manila papers. Be sure that at least one member of the municipal planning team is there to assist one barangay in the course of this exercise.

After 4 hours (240 minutes), call a last plenary for purposes of presenting the outputs, by barangay, to key development stakeholders and actors. The latter would include, among others, the municipal mayor, vice mayor, Sangguniang Bayan members, congressional representative, responsible officers of line agencies of government which are critical to enterprise promotion and development, local NGO representatives, local banks' representatives and other potential funding or resource agencies. To them, the enterprise development plans, by sector and barangay, are presented for purposes of validation and to elicit their informed comments and suggestions. Most of all, these are presented for purposes of generating their commitments of support. In this context, the presentation becomes as it were a pledging session.

To ensure their presence, the municipal government writes letters of invitation. Handcarry these letters, as early as possible, to the official addressees so that immediate commitment can be obtained and the official representatives identified for inclusion in the programme.

Be sure to document the proceedings of the presentation. Likewise, make a synthesis of the proceedings, giving emphasis on the comments, suggestions and commitments of support that may have been made. Never forget to thank the guests you invited, the LGU sponsor and the workshop participants, especially, for taking active part in all the planning processes.

Retrieve all outputs after the presentation. Advise the participants that their sectoral plans shall be consolidated by the Municipal Planning Team into Barangay Enterprise Development Plans (BEDPs), a printed copy of which shall be made available later for their use. The BEDPs, in turn, are integrated into the Municipal Enterprise Development Plan, a process that is discussed in the next chapter.

Exhibits 19-20 show some hypothetical samples of Sectoral Enterprise Development Plans.

Time Requirement

This process requires at most 7 hours (420 minutes): 4 hours to draft the sectoral plans and 3 hours to present these.

Required Materials, Supplies and Equipment

The following are needed for this process:

Outputs from Exercises 3 (Barangay vision, Chapter 6) & 5 (Feasible opportunities, Chapter 7) on manila papers posted on the blackboard or wall;
Sectoral planning formats/outlines written on the blackboard or on manila paper posted on the blackboard or wall;
Manila papers; Pentel pens;

Scotch or paper tapes; Ball pens;

Yellow pad papers and bond papers;

Transparencies and transparency pens (if electricity is available in the area);

Blackboard and chalk or whiteboard and markers;

Overhead projector, if available and practicable; and

Computer and printer, if available and practicable.

Exhibit 20
Sample Enterprise Development Plan for Women Sec tor

I. Identifying Information

	A.	Sector	Women
	B.	Barangay	Miaray
	C.	Municipality & Province	Dangcagan, Bukidnon
II.	**Local Resource Base**		
	A.	Natural	200 hectares coconut
	B.	Human	100 unemployed wives
III.	**Preferred Livelihood**		Coco Food Processing
IV.	**Product**		Coco Vinegar
V.	**Business Organization Form**		Cooperative
VI.	**Objectives**		

A.	Develop men t Objectives		
	1.	Household income	Increased household income fro m Php 1,500 a month to Php 5,000 a month beginning in 2005.
	2.	Employment	100 wives shall have been self-employed by end of 2005.
B.	Business Objectives		
	1.	Sales	At least Php 60,000 per month beginning in 2005.
	2.	Market share	5% to 10 % of provincial market is captured by end of 2007.
	3.	Profit	An annual return on investment of 30 %.

VII. Strategies

A.	Product Strategy	Project the product as a natural, chemical-free vinegar from the tree of life. Brand and package the product in properly sealed bottles.
B.	Place/Distribution Strategy	Utilize such provincial outlets as groceries, malls, sari-sari stores, hotels and restaurants, hospitals, etc. Explore possibility of producing for established companies as Datu Puti, Amihan and other vinegar manufacturers.
C.	Price Strategy	Sell at prices prevailing.

VIII. Implementation Plan

	Activity	Time Frame			Responsibility
		Y_0	Y_1	Y_{2-5}	
A.	Discuss business opportunity w/ unemployed wives				Principal Proponent
B.	If at least 15 are interested, organize into a cooperative: ➢ Ask help of Municipal Agriculturist Office (MAO) for conduct of pre-membership seminar (PMS). ➢ Hold seminar ➢ Collect membership dues ➢ Register coop with CDA				Principal Proponent w/ support of members
C.	Ask help of Mayor's Office for the conduct of applied training on vinegar-making, simplified bookkeeping and business management, among others.				Chair Person General Manager

D.	Build up capital					General Manager Treasurer
E.	Source additional capital					General Manager
F.	Set up business and operationalize					General Manager Management Staff
G.	Monitor and assess					General Manager Management Staff

IX. Financial Requirements

	Item		Factor	Cost (Php)
A.	Capital Costs			
	1.	Equipment	Lump sum	10,000
		Sub-Total		10,000
B.	W orking Capital			
	1.	Direct materials	Php3,000/mo. x 3 mos.	9,000
	2.	Operating expenses	Php5,000/ month x 3 mos.	15,000
		Sub-Total		24,000
C.	Pre-operating Expenses			
	1.	Organizational exp.		2,000
	2.	Registration		1,000
		Sub-Total		3,000
		Total		37,000

X. Financing Plan

	Item	Total	Coop	Grant
A.	Capital costs	10,000	8,000	2,000
B.	Working capital	24,000	4,800	19,200
C.	Pre-operating exp.	3,000	3,000	0
	Total	37,000	15,800	21,200
	Ratio	100	42.7	57.3

Exhibit 21
Sample Sectoral Enterprise Development Plan for LGU Sector

I. Identifying Information

A.	Sector	LGU
B.	Barangay	Bislig
C.	Municipality & Province	Tanauan, Leyte
II.	**Local Resource Base**	
	A. Natural	2000 hectares of land planted to various crops
	B. Human	500 residents with various trade skills
III.	**Preferred Mission**	➢ Provision of Enterprise Support Facilities ➢ Enforcement of environmental protection laws
IV.	**Products**	➢ Passable road network ➢ Trading center ➢ Legislations in support to enterprise development ➢ Mangrove plantation
V.	**Organizational Form**	Corporation

VI. Development Objectives

1.	Household income	Increased household income for at least 50 rural families from Php1,500 to Php5,000 a month by end of 2005.
2.	Employment	50 new jobs shall have been created by end of 2005.
3.	Environmental protection & rehabilitation	➢ Incidence of illegal fishing and astray animals reduced by 70% beginning in 2005. ➢ 50 hectares of mangroves are reforested by end of 2006. ➢ Ordinance banning astray animals is passed & enforced by end of 2005.
4.	Accessibility	5 km of road network made passable by end of 2005.
5.	Enterprise support facility	A trading center for farm and fish products shall been set up by end of 2005.

VII. Strategies

A.	Resource mobilization	Seek funding assistance for infrastructure and mangrove rehabilitation projects from prospective donors (e.g., municipal government, provincial government, congressional district, from friendly senators and party list representatives, and the DENR).
B.	Information & education campaigns	Organize and conduct community consultations for purposes of getting the people to cooperate in the observance of environmental laws.
C.	Local hiring of workers for infrastructure projects	Convince the contractors or project engineers to source workers locally.

VIII. Implementation Plan

Activity		Time Frame			Responsibility
		Y_0	Y_1	Y_{2-5}	
A.	Prepare project proposals for prospective donors or engage services of a technical man to prepare proposals				Barangay Council
B.	Ask the Municipal Mayor or any higher authority to endorse proposals to prospective donors				Barangay Council
C.	Send proposals to prospective funders				Barangay Captain
D.	Follow up proposals with prospective donors				Barangay Captain
E.	If funds for projects are made available by donors, meet with contractors and convince them to hire workers locally				Barangay Captain
F.	Monitor progress of project implementation				Barangay Council

IX. Financial Requirements

	Item	Factor	Cost (Php)
A.	Proposal preparation	3 proposals x Php1,000/proposal	3,000
	Sub-Total		3,000
B.	Communications		500
	Sub-Total		500
C.	Transport/travel	Php500/month x 12 mos.	6,000
	Sub-Total		6,000
	Total		9,500

Chapter 9

Integration

Objective

This final phase seeks to integrate the BEDPs into what is now the Municipal Enterprise Development Plan (MEDP).

Required Materials, Supplies and Equipment

Secure the following outputs and materials for this activity:

- Summary of findings from environmental scanning and analysis;
- Summary of opportunities and threats, and strengths and weakness of the barangay councils;
- Summary of feasible opportunities identified during the barangay planning workshops;
- Vision and mission statements of the barangays;
- Vision and mission statements of the LGU, if any;
- Sample vision and mission statements;
- Overhead projector;
- Transparencies and transparency pens;
- Manila papers;
- Scotch or paper tapes;
- Metacards;
- Yellow pad, bond papers and ball pens;
- Blackboard and chalk or whiteboard and whiteboard markers;
- Sound system; and
- Computer and printer.

Process

Organize a 1-day to 1.5-day's workshop, preferably live-in, to achieve the following:

- Identify the strengths and weaknesses of the municipal government;
- Identify the core values of the LGU key people; and
- Formulate or revisit and refine the municipal vision, mission and objectives, if these have been formulated.

Participants in this workshop are key LGU officers. They would include: the municipal mayor; vice mayor; heads of offices; municipal councilors; local NGO representatives; and members of the municipal development council. Thirty (30) participants at most would constitute a manageable number. Prepare a formal programme for this workshop.

For LGUs that are first timers in this exercise, it is always wise to engage the professional services of an external organization development specialist to serve as workshop facilitator.

Presentation of Findings from Environmental Scanning (30 minutes)

After the usual program opening, introduction, expectation-setting and leveling off, begin the activity with a report on the progress of the planning exercise. Present the salient findings from the barangay planning workshops. Give emphasis on the results of environmental analyses made: the opportunities and threats, and the strengths and weaknesses of the barangay LGUs. Finally, let them know of what still need to be done to complete the MEDP process.

Allow a 10-minute open forum for possible questions, reactions to the information generated so far, clarifications or additional insights. Thereafter, introduce the first workshop and what it hopes to accomplish.

Workshop # 1: Organizational Analysis (80 minutes)

Break the participants into groups, by office. The following groupings will do: (1) Mayor's Office; (2) Municipal Agricultural Office; (3) Municipal Health Office; (4) Municipal Social Welfare & Development Office; (5) Municipal Planning and Development Office; (6) Municipal Engineer's Office; (7) Civil Registrar's Office; (8) General Services Office); (9) Treasurer's Office; (10) Municipal Accountant's Office; (11) Budget Office; and (12) Sangguniang Bayan.

Then, ask the groups to do the following:

> *Identify the strengths and weaknesses of your office with respect to the performance of its mandate. Suggest what need be done to address its weaknesses. Write your findings and recommendations on manila papers using pentel pens.*

After 20 minutes, call a plenary. Give each group 5 minutes to present their output. Make a synthesis of the findings and recommendations after the presentations. Emphasize the significance of the information gathered: as critical inputs to the formulation of strategies towards the sustainable development of the municipality.

Workshop # 2: Core Values Identification (15 minutes)

This activity is conducted in the same manner as the one undergone by the participants in the barangay planning workshops (refer to Chapter 5, Value Analysis).

Give out 3 metacards and a pentel pen to each participant and ask them to do the following in 5 minutes:

> *In one word, name at most 3 things that you believe*
> *in or love most. Don't argue. Write each word on a*
> *separate metacard. When you finish, paste your cards*
> *to the manila paper provided on the board.*

After 5 minutes, combine the similarities and clarify the values put forward. Close the workshop with a synthesis, stressing the significance of core values in crafting the municipal vision. Keep these core values posted elsewhere after the exercise because the participants would need to refer to these in the succeeding activity.

Workshop # 3: Vision-Setting

Crafting the Vision (80 minutes)

Essentially the same visioning procedure undertaken in the barangay planning workshops is followed at this level.

Do not break the participants into smaller groups for this exercise. In this manner, they re-visit the vision collectively and re-state it collectively, too. In so doing, consensus can happen faster: a feat hardly attainable when there is more than one version to consider. Begin the exercise by asking the participants to do the following:

> *In clear and simple language, describe what you want*
> *to become as an LGU, as a municipality, as a people*
> *and as employees 10-20 years from now. Write your*
> *vision statement legibly on manila paper.*

To hasten this exercise, distribute—for reference—enough copies of abridged materials on visioning, and elements and characteristics of a good vision discussed at length in Chapter 5. Also provide enough copies of one or two model vision statements. If ready, distribute as well the vision statements of the various barangays so that these can be captured in the municipal vision. Advise the group to refer to their core values, their opportunities and threats, and their strengths and weaknesses.

After an hour, ask the group to present their work. Subject the output to scrutiny by posing such questions as:

> Does it reflect your core values and the barangay people's?
> Does it capture what the municipality is capable of becoming given its resource endowments, its economic opportunities and threats, and the strengths and weaknesses of the LGU as a development organization?
> Does it motivate and inspire commitment to action?
> Do you experience goose pimples just reading it?
> Is it simple, clear, achievable and enduring enough?

Close the exercise with a synthesis, stressing the function of an organizational vision (i.e., a motivating, inspiring, and compelling force to action), its critical elements and the need to craft this in a way that would inspire and compel a community to action. Produce enough printed copies of the vision statement and distribute to each participant. Post a copy in a conspicuous area for everyone to read or refer to.

Revisiting the Vision (60 minutes)

This is done when the municipal LGU has an existing vision statement. Produce enough printed copies of the vision statement and distribute these to each participant. Without breaking the participants into smaller groups, start the revisit exercise by asking the group to answer the following questions:

- Do you feel like holding on to this vision? Does it reflect your core values?
- Does it capture what the municipality is capable of becoming given its resource endowments, its economic opportunities

and threats, and the strengths and weaknesses of the LGU as an organization? Does it motivate and inspire commitment to action?

- Is it simple, clear, concrete, attainable?
- If you had to re-state your vision, what would it be like?

Also make available to the participants enough materials on visioning, the critical elements and characteristics of a good vision statement, including some models that they could refer to. Likewise, make available, if ready, the visions crafted by the barangays so that these may be captured in the municipal vision.

After 45 minutes, call a plenary and ask a volunteer to present the vision statement. Thereafter, ask the group if this reflects all that they want to become as an LGU, as a municipality and as a people. Make the necessary changes or additions to the statement when called for. Close this exercise by providing the same synthesis suggested above.

Workshop # 4: Mission-Setting

Crafting the Municipal Mission (80 minutes)

Begin the exercise by asking them to do the following as a group:

> *What role do you think should your LGU play to realize your vision? How would you put this mission in words? Copy your mission statement legibly on manila paper.*

To help the group crystallize what mission is most appropriate for the LGU, pose the following questions:

- What is your LGU's reason for being as defined in the Local
- Government Code?

- Who are your customers or constituents? What are you good at?
- What are you weak at?
- What values hold you together?

In addition, provide the group copies of some model mission that they can refer to, such as Calbiga's quoted in Chapter 6. Advise them to revisit their core values, vision, and their strengths and weaknesses as a development organization

After an hour, ask the group to present the mission statement they crafted together. Ask the participants to scrutinize their own work by posing such questions as:

- Will your mission effectively fulfill your vision?
- Is it congruent to your legal mandate or your reason for being? Does it reflect your core values, and what you are good and weak at?
- Does it clarify who your customers are?
- Does it provide a framework for developing objectives and strategy, defining critical success factors, and making resource allocation choices?
- Does it evoke feeling and passion, and personal response?

Ask the group to make the necessary changes as they see fit. Reproduce printed copies of the mission statement.

Revisiting the Mission (60 minutes)

Do this in case the municipal LGU has an existing mission statement. Begin by asking the participants, as a group, following questions:

- *Do you feel your mission can effectively fulfill your vision?*
- *If you had to re-state your mission, what would it be like?*

Provide the group the same aid materials and pose the same aid questions as those singled out in the foregoing sub-section.

After 45 minutes, ask the group to copy their work on manila paper and present this. Thereafter, ask them to scrutinize their mission statement by posing the same questions asked in the preceding section. Advise them to make changes as they see fit. Close the exercise by a synthesis on the critical elements and characteristics of an effective mission statement.

Writing the Plan

This final activity involves the packaging of the Municipal Enterprise Development Plan, with the BEDPs and the wealth of experience of the planning team members as major inputs.

There is no standard format to follow in writing the MEDP. Styles vary according to the taste of the plan writer or writers. In any case, the written plan should be able to capture what it is: a master plan to guide the LGU, particularly those involved in managing the economic development of the municipality, in the task of attaining sustainable development.

Presented purely as a suggested outline, the one shown on Exhibit 22 departs a great deal from the first MEDP report written by the author. The revisions are deemed necessary to add more substance and coherence to the plan. Chapter 10 provides a detailed guide to writing the plan according to this outline.

Exhibit 22
A Suggested MEDP Report Outline

Foreword by Municipal Mayor
Acknowledgments
Table of Contents
List of Tables
List of Exhibits List of Figures
Introduction Executive Summary

Part 1 Planning Considerations

Chapter 1 Resource Assessment

Natural Resources
Total Land Area and Land-use
Topography
Soils, Climate and Rainfall
Major Crops and Livestock
Prices Received by Farmers
Aqua-Marine Resources
Food Production and Consumption
Cereals
Meat Products
Fish Products
Vegetables
Fruits
Major Commodity Flows
Tourist Attractions
Other Major Resources

Human Resources
Population Trends
Number of Households and Trends
Population, by Age Group
Population, by Sex
Population, by Educational Attainment
Population, by Religious Affiliation
Population, by Ethnic Origin and Dialect
Labor Force and Employment
Labor Force and Employment
Technical and Vocational Skills
Household Income and Expenditures
Poverty Incidence and Poverty Sectors

Institutional Resources
  Government Institutions
  Non-Government Organizations
  Banks
  Foreign Governments
  Others

Internal Resources
  Development
  Fund Local Revenues Infrastructure Facilities
  Machinery and Equipment
  Real Estate Holdings
  Internal Expertise and Competencies
  Others

Enterprise Opportunities
Environmental Threats

Chapter 2 Enterprise Assessment

Enterprise Preferences
  Agriculture and Fisheries Sector
  Trade and Industry Sector
  Services Sector
  Tourism Sector

Feasible Opportunities
  Selection Criteria
  Feasible Enterprises
    Agriculture and Fisheries Sector
    Trade and Industry Sector
    Services Sector
    Tourism Sector (if applicable)

Part 2 The Municipal Enterprise Development Plan

Chapter 3 Enterprise Development Plan Framework
  Municipal Vision
  Mission
  Objectives

Chapter 4 Strategic Options
  Agriculture and Fisheries Sector
  Trade and Industry Sector
  Services Sector
  Tourism Sector (if applicable)

Chapter 5 Strategic Interventions
Credit Assistance Program
Infrastructure Support Program
Capacity-Building Program
Marketing Assistance Program
Environmental Management Program
Other Interventions

Chapter 6 Plan Implementation Arrangements

Chief Implementation Unit
Personnel Requirements
Implementation Schedule

Chapter 7 Financing Requirements and Financing Plan

Total Financing Requirements
Financing Plan

Chapter 8 Plan Monitoring and Evaluation

Monitoring and Evaluation System
Monitoring & Evaluation Team

Appendices

Chapter 10

Guide to Writing the Plan

"Brevity is the soul of wit."
William Shakespeare

Writing the plan is a task that most, if not all, planners find so laborious, if not daunting. Even with an outline to go by, there is always the anxiety that comes from not being confident about what information to include or exclude in a section or subsection of the report.

To lessen the anxiety and pains associated with report writing, this chapter is added to this handbook to provide a detailed guide to writing each section and sub-section of the Municipal Enterprise Development Plan. Reference, however, is made to the suggested outline shown on Exhibit 21 (Chapter 9).

Foreword

This page, usually written and signed by the Mayor, briefly introduces the plan, stresses its significance and invites local and external entrepreneurs to exploit the investment opportunities that the municipality has to offer.

Acknowledgments

Also one page at most, this portion usually follows the Foreword or Preface. Some authors, though, prefer to locate this ahead of the Foreword and that's their prerogative. By its very title, this part of the report acknowledges the invaluable assistance of all individuals, farmers' groups, fishers' groups, women's groups, out-of-school youth, business people, offices, institutions and agencies who, in one way or another, contributed to the drafting of the plan. If enumerating them all will cover more than a page, it is wise to allot a page or two for this purpose in the appendix.

Executive Summary

This portion, preferably no more than five pages, should be able to capture the following information:

1. What are the objectives of the plan?
2. How does it hope to achieve these objectives? What strategic interventions are envisioned?
3. What mechanism is proposed to anchor local enterprise promotion and development?
4. How much will it cost to implement the plan?
5. How does it propose to finance plan implementation?

Introduction

This section may be broken into three sub-sections: (1) Objectives of the Plan; (2) Methodology; and (3) Limitations.

The first introduces the general objectives of the plan, that is to say, the reasons behind the need to draft the plan. These objectives may be stated, as follows:

to promote the sustainable development of the municipality;
to provide local and external investors with information on the investment opportunities that the municipality has to offer; and

to guide the LGU in the implementation, monitoring and evaluation of the plan.

The second presents in reasonable detail the methodology used in the formulation of the plan.

And the third discusses briefly the limitation(s) of the plan. Among others, it cautions the readers that the investments identified in the plan have not been subjected to feasibility studies and, therefore, cannot be used as strong basis for the making of a more rational investment decision.

Part 1 Planning Considerations

This part provides the premises or the logic of the plan and consists of the first two chapters of the report, the contents of which are discussed in turn below.

Chapter 1 Resource Assessment

This chapter presents the salient findings from the analysis of the external and the internal environment, in a manner that exposes the opportunities and threats in the external environment, and the strengths and weaknesses of the LGU as an organization. Below are guide points to writing the various sections and subsections of this chapter.

Natural Resources

Total Land Area and General Land-Use

Present the municipal land area and its breakdown into various land uses (e.g., agricultural area, forest lands, swamps and grasslands, residential area, commercial area, industrial area, institutional area).

Topography

The terrain of a development area necessarily shapes its suitability with respect to agricultural activities and the choice of technology. Describe the general terrain or slope characteristics of the municipality. The municipal topographic map, usually available at the Municipal Engineer's Office or the Municipal Planning and Development Office, is a good source of data on this.

Describe the topography of the municipality according to its slope classes, if data are available. Class A (0-3% slope) terrain is level to nearly level; Class B (3-8% slope) is gently sloping; Class C (8-18% slope) is gently undulating and gently rolling; Class D (1-30% slope) is moderately undulating and rolling; and Class E (over 30% slope) is steeply undulating and rolling.

Information on the area covered by each slope class is critical for purposes of identifying agricultural investments appropriate to each slope class, including the alternative technologies appropriate to each slope class. Show this information in a statistical table. If no technical data are available, describe the topography qualitatively.

Soil, Climate and Rainfall

The climatic and soil characteristics of an area also influence a great deal its suitability to specific agricultural activities and the choice of technology. Describe the type of climate that the municipality belongs to (e.g., Type I, II, III, IV). Describe the rainy and dry months and the average annual rainfall during the last 10 years. If the municipality is located within the typhoon belt, provide information on the number of typhoons passing through the area each year and the typhoon months.

Characterize the types of soil present in the municipality, including the corresponding area covered by each soil type. The Office of Municipal Agriculturist should be able to provide this information. If not, the Bureau of Soils of the Department of Agriculture will surely have this information. If available, show the climatological and soil maps in this section. Also show a table on rainfall data obtained from the nearest Pagasa station.

Major Crops and Livestock

Single out the *major* crops and livestock produced by the municipality. Information in this regard can be lifted from the Barangay Enterprise Development Plans. Characterize each major crop as to area devoted to it; the number of families dependent on it; the local product or products currently made from the resource; its productive capacity in terms of yield per ha vis-à-vis the provincial and national yield levels; its planting and harvesting calendar; the future uses or products that can still be derived from the resource; and the current status, problems or constraints confronting the resource. The latter may involve markets, support infrastructures, access to financing, ownership/tenure, technology, or environmental degradation.

Similarly, characterize each major livestock/poultry as to population; estimated number of families engaged in each type of livestock/poultry; the product or products currently derived from the resource; the current status, problems or constraints confronting the resource; and the future uses or products that can still be derived from the resource.

Present these data as much as possible in statistical tables.

Prices Received by Farmers

Present in statistical table the average prices received by farmers for major products marketed. A description of how prices received by farmers are set would be useful in defining the necessary marketing intervention.

Aqua-Marine Resources

These resources include the municipal coastal waters, inland fishponds, rivers, springs, lakes, coral reefs, artificial reefs and mangroves.

Characterize each resource as to size (e.g., nautical mile; hectare; kilometer; number; etc.); number of households or barangays dependent on each resource; its current uses or the products that the people derive from each; its current productive capacity today vis-à-vis its potentials or its previous years' productive performance; the potential products that can still be derived; and the present status, problems or constraints confronting each resource. Information on the environmental status of these resources would be useful in designing appropriate interventions towards their rehabilitation and protection, as the case may be.

Food Production and Consumption

This subsection, which may be subdivided into cereals, meat products, fish products, vegetables and fruits, presents a comparative description of the local food production and consumption requirements for purposes of determining whether the locality is a surplus or a deficit area in basic food products. Information in this regard would be useful in designing production interventions in case of production shortfalls, or marketing interventions in case of production surpluses.

Estimate consumption requirements using the latest average per capita consumption figures of the Bureau of Agricultural Statistics (BAS) which conducts periodic consumption surveys. Per capita consumption is simply multiplied by the total population to get an estimate of consumption requirements. The resulting figure is then compared with production, net of quantities that go to seeds, feeds and wastage, to determine whether there exists a surplus or shortfall. For major products as cereals, vegetable and fruits, estimates of average wastage or losses and quantities used for seeds and feeds are available at the BAS.

Major Commodity Flows

This subsection describes how the municipality's major products are disposed. Present percentage estimates of the output that goes to the market and to home consumption. Describe where the surplus production goes (i.e., geographic markets) and how these surpluses are moved (e.g., by local traders, by *viajeros*, etc.). If possible, show a commodity flow diagram.

Tourist Attractions

If any tourist spots are present within the municipality, characterize each as to size; distinct features; current uses; its enterprise development potentials; and the status and problems confronting the resource. As much as possible, show pictures of these tourist attractions.

Other Major Resources

Single out and characterize other major resources of the municipality, if any.

Human Resources

Population Trends

Present in a statistical table the latest population count for the municipality, by barangay. Describe the annual growth rate of the municipal population; this information can be obtained from the National Statistics Office (NSO) or the National Statistical Coordination Board (NSCB). Provide projections of the municipal population during the next 10 years and present these in a statistical table.

Number of Households and Trends

Present estimates in statistical tables of the current number of households in the municipality and the household population, by barangay. The average household size can be estimated by dividing the household population by the number of households.

Describe the trend in the number of households by comparing the figures between two or three censal periods. It is increasing or decreasing? The trend can be determined by computing for the annual growth rate over two, three or even four censal periods using a common formula as:

Annual Growth Rate = (Number of Households in 2000/Number of Households in 1995)$^{1/t}$—1

Where:
t = the number of years
between censal years
(i.e., 2000-1995), and
1 = constant.

With the use of a computer software as Microsoft Excel, it is pretty easy to arrive at the average annual growth rate figure.

Present projections of the number of households during the next 10 years. These are available at the NSO or NSCB. If not, projections into the future can be made using the annual growth rate figure.

Population by Age Groups

Describe the distribution of the municipal population according to age groups. This can be presented in a frequency distribution table. Age groups represent market segments and, by their proportions, entrepreneurs would be interested in knowing which age groups to penetrate. Trends in age group distribution can be established by comparing data between censal periods.

Distribution by age groups can be projected into the future by using the computed average annual growth rate figures, by age group. But this method can be laborious considering the number of age groups. An easier alternative is to project the distribution from the projected total population on the assumption that the percentage distributions in the last censal year will stay the same. Present the projected population, by age group, in a statistical table.

Population by Sex

Information on proportions of males and females is of interest to the entrepreneur for purposes of market segmentation.

Describe the distribution of the municipal population according to sex. Which is the more dominant population: male or female? Present the population, by sex, in a statistical table.

Describe the trends in the male and female population by comparing the distributions during the last three or four censal periods. Has there been a change in the proportion of females with respect to the males?

Project the male and female population over the next 10 years, assuming the percentage distribution in the last censal year would stay the same. Multiply these percentages by the projected municipal population to get an estimate of the projected male or female population. Present the projections in a statistical table.

Population by Educational Level

The educational characteristics of a development area are important to the entrepreneur in many ways. If the population is highly educated and skilled, the investor may not have to seek elsewhere for the skills and the professionals he or she needs. On the other hand, a generally low educational level may encourage the entrepreneur or a social development agency to invest in educational projects intended to improve educational levels.

Present in a statistical table the municipal population, by educational level. Information in this regard can be obtained from the census of population published by the NSO or the NSCB. Describe the level of education attained by the broad majority of the municipal population. Using the age group distribution data, project the number of school age population over the next 10 years.

Information on the school population is useful in projecting classroom requirements and in making decisions on what educational products to sell to this market segment.

Population by Religious Affiliation

Information on the religious characteristics of a development area is also important to the entrepreneur. A predominantly catholic population, for instance, would give the entrepreneur an idea of what religious products to develop or to move to this market segment. On the other hand, a predominantly Baptist population would tell an entrepreneur that a pork production business is a no-no with respect to this market.

Describe the distribution of the municipal population according to religious affiliation. This information can be presented in a frequency distribution table. Latest data on religious characteristics can be obtained from the NSO or NSCB, particularly from the latest population census.

Population by Ethnic Origin and Dialect

Information on population distribution by ethnic origin and dialect is useful to the entrepreneur. For instance, a predominantly Cebuano population would likely prefer corn to rice as staple food, or a *Cebuano* tabloid to one using *Tagalog* as medium.

Describe the population according to the presence and proportions of ethnic groupings, with emphasis on the most dominant ethnic groups and dialects. Present the data in a statistical table.

Labor Force and Employment

The labor force refers to the population 15 years old and over. Not all of those belonging to this age bracket, however, are members of the labor force for reasons that many are in school, too old to work or have disabilities that virtually keep them out of the labor market.

Describe the municipal labor force according to sex and employment status, by economic sector (i.e., agriculture and fisheries; trade and industry; services), if data are available. Present this information in a statistical table. Data in this regard can be obtained from the census of population published by the NSO.

Describe the trends in labor force size by comparing available data during the last three or four censal periods. Compute for the average annual growth rate. Using this growth rate, project the labor force, by sex, during the next 10 years. Present the projections in a statistical table.

Information on labor force characteristics is critical to the formulation of LGU objectives around a key result area as *employment*.

Technical and Vocational Skills

Single out the technical and vocational skills present in the locality, as generated from the barangay planning workshops. Characterize each skill as to the number of skilled residents; their employment status; estimated size of local market; the quality of each skill as indicated by the quality of product or service produced; and the problems or constraints confronting the skilled residents.

Information on skills availability is useful in designing livelihood activities around these skills. At the micro or enterprise level, it is useful in the making of decisions on skills sourcing.

Household Income and Expenditures

For obvious reasons, information on average household income and expenditures is critical to the social development planners (i.e., LGU, line agencies of government, NGOs and other donor agencies) as well as the entrepreneur. To the local government, information on household income and expenditures across all social sectors is critical in many respects. With it, the local government and other social development agencies can identify which social sectors are impoverished and which are affluent. With it, the LGU is, thus, able to design the appropriate interventions or strategies to alleviate poverty.

On the other hand, to the entrepreneur, information on household income and expenditures is useful in terms of deciding on what products and services to engage in and in targeting the market segments to penetrate.

There is currently no statistical agency that collects and publishes municipal level data on income and expenditures. The NSO periodically collects and releases household income, expenditures and savings data, but estimates are available only at the provincial level. To generate information in this regard is to conduct sample household income and expenditure surveys. Should budgetary constraints stand in the way, case studies across the major social sectors may be conducted for purposes of getting indicative estimates.

Describe the major income sources of the municipal households, and the average household income and expenditures levels of various social sectors (e.g., farmers, fisherfolk, professionals, employed labor sector, etc.).

Poverty Incidence and Poverty Sectors

Identify which social sectors are impoverished by comparing the average household income, by social sector, vis-à-vis the regional or provincial poverty threshold estimate of the NSO or the National Economic Development Authority. Present the average household income and expenditures data in a statistical table.

Institutional Resources

Government Institutions

Our review of the institutional environment should be able to identify the government institutions external to the LGU, which have resources to offer for the development of the municipality. These would include the provincial government; national government; house of representatives; senate; government financing institutions as the Land Bank of the Philippines, Development Bank of the Philippines, Quedan Corporation, National Livelihood Support Fund and others; and line agencies of government. Single out the institutions which are more likely to give access to the LGU and characterize each institution as to its mandate, priorities in terms of livelihood activities to support, and the resources (e.g., financing; technology; materials; equipment) it has to offer in support to enterprise development.

Non-Government Organizations

Likewise, single out the non-government institutions such as NGOs, local banks, and universities and colleges which more likely to give access to the LGU. Characterize each institution as to its mandate, priorities in terms of livelihood activities to support, and the resources (e.g., financing; technology; materials; equipment) it has to offer in support to enterprise development.

Private Banks

Single out the nearest private banks which are likely to offer financing in support of the municipal enterprise development plan. Describe briefly the credit facilities they offer.

Foreign Governments

Foreign governments through their embassies or development agencies in the Philippines are also potential sources of various resources. If any, single out the institutions which you think the LGU can most likely go to for any form of assistance and characterize each as to mandate, priorities in terms of livelihood activities to support, and resources to offer.

Internal Resources

Finally, single out the resources of the LGU which can be utilized for enterprise promotion and development. These would include its annual development fund; local revenues; infrastructure facilities; machinery and equipment; real estate holdings; and internal expertise and competencies.

Characterize each resource according to size (e.g., amount; length; number; area); quality; and its status and problems. The latter information indicates the LGU's weaknesses and would be critical in the design of interventions to address these.

Enterprise Opportunities

A picture of the various livelihood opportunities, which can be lifted from the Barangay Enterprise Development Plans with additional inputs from the municipal planning team, provides the highlight of this chapter. Present the enterprise opportunities in a summary matrix such as the one shown on Exhibit 23 below.

Exhibit 23
En terprise Opportunities, by Barangay

Barangay	Most Significant Resource		Enterprise Opportunity	Target Product or Service
	Name	Size		
A	Irrigated area	200 hectares (ha)	Palay production	Palay
	Other lowland area	100 ha	Vegetable production	Beans Onions
			Orchard	Banana
	Palay	1,440 m.t. per year	Rice milling	Milled rice Rice bran
	Banana	200 m.t. per year	Banana processing	Banana chips
	Coconut	420,000 nuts per year	Integrated coconut processing	Coconut oil Co co coir Geotextile Coco charcoal Coco vinegar
B	Mangrove area	500 ha	Mudcrab production	Mudcrab Crablets
	Bay area	5 kilometers	Seaweed production	Carageenan

			Fish production in cages	Lapu-lapu Fingerlings
	Ub e	500 m.t. per year	Food processing	Ub e jam
	Ticog	10 ha	Mat we aving	Sleeping mats Placemats
	Bamboo	20 ha	Furniture mak ing	Sala sets Chairs
C	Computer technicians	5 people	Computer shop	Computer assembly Computer repairs, etc.

Environmental Threats

Likewise, a summary of environmental threats provides salient information to cap this chapter. Information on environmental threats is crucial to the making of final enterprise or livelihood choices as well as the design of interventions needed to address the threats. Single these out and discuss each of these threats briefly. Among others, environmental threats may include environmental degradation (e.g., soil erosion or runoffs; illegal fishing methods; illegal logging; harmful mining operations); government policies inimical to small enterprise development; and peace and order.

Chapter 2 Enterprise Assessment

This chapter presents the results of value analysis and the matching process discussed in Chapter 6 and Chapter 7, respectively. The chapter may be developed according to the following sections.

Enterprise Preferences, by Social Sector

Summarize this section in matrices such as those shown on Exhibits 24-29.

Exhibit 24

Farming Sector: Enterprise Preferences, by Barangay

Most Significant Resource & Size	Enterprise Preference	Target Product or Service	Barangay
Irrigated area (200 ha) Lowland area (100 ha)	Palay production Vegetable production	Palay Lettuce Potato Bell pepper	A, B, C D, E, F
Bay area (15 km.)	Banana production Fish production in cages	Saba Lapu-lapu Fingerlings	D, E, F G, H, I, J

Exhibit 25

Women Sector: Enterprises Preferences, by Barangay

Most Significant Resource & Size	Enterprise Preference	Target Product or Service	Barangay
All species of fish (200 m.t. per year)	Fish vending	All fish species	G, H, I, J
Saba (150 m.t. per year)	Food processing	Banana chips Banana cue Banana cake	K, L, M
Skilled dressmakers (20 women)	Tailoring	Students' uniforms Children's clothes	Poblacion
Beauticians (10 persons)	Beauty shop	Hair-cut Manicure Pedicure Make-up	Poblacion

Exhibit 26
Out of School Youth Sector: Enterprises Preferences, by Barangay

Most Significant Resource & Size	Enterprise Preference	Target Product or Service	Barangay
Bamboo plantation (120 ha)	Furniture production	Bamboo sala sets Bamboo chairs	A, B, C, D, E, F
Computer technicians (5 persons)	Computer shop	Computer assembly Computer repairs Encoding & printing	Poblacion
Guitarists (4 persons) Drummers (2 persons) Singers (5 persons)	Live band	Entertainment	Poblacion

Exhibit 27
Fishing Sector: Enterprises Preferences, by Barangay

Most Significant Resource & Size	Enterprise Preference	Target Product or Service	Barangay
100 ha mangrove area	Mudcrab production	Mudcrab Crablets	G, H, I, J
100 ha Bay area	Fish production in cages	Lapu-lapu Fingerlings	G, H, I, J
	Seaweeds production	Carageenan	G, H, I, J

Exhibit 28
Business Sector: Enterprises Preferences, by Barangay

Most Significant Resource & Size	Enterprise Preference	Target Product or Service	Barangay
200 m.t. palay production per year	Rice milling	Milled rice Rice bran	A, B, C
2 million coconuts per year	Integrated coconut processing	Coconut oil Coco coir Coco charcoal Geotextile Coco vinegar	G, H, I, J

Exhibit 29

Local Government Sector: Enterprises Preferences, by Barangay

Most Significant Resource & Size	Enterprise Preference	Target Product or Service	Barangay
10 ha real estate property	Expansion of public market	Market stalls	Poblacion
Cathedral caves	Eco-tourism	Guided tours Souvenir items	Panayuran
Spring (1000 gallons per minute)	Water supply system	Portable water	Murok-burok

Feasible Opportunities

This section presents the sectoral livelihood preferences considered feasible according to certain selection criteria. Begin by discussing briefly the criteria including the rating system. Then present the feasible opportunities in a matrix as the one shown on Exhibit 29 below.

Exhibit 29

Feasible Enterprise Opportunities, by Economic Sector, by Barangay

	Feasible Opportunity	Target Product or Service	Enterprise Category*	Location (Barangay)	No. of Enterprise
50	**Agriculture & Fisheries Sector**				
50	Palay production	Palay	Micro	A, B, C	150
A.	**Agriculture & Fisheries Sector**				
2.	Vegetable production	Lettuce Potato Bell pepper	Micro	D, E, F	50
3.	Banana production	Banana	Micro	D, E, F	100
4.	Cattle production	Live cattle	Micro		

5.	Mudcrab production	Mudcrab Crablets	Micro	G, H, I, J	
6.	Fish production in cages	Lapu-lapu Fingerlings	Micro	G, H, I, J	80
B.	**Trade & Industry Sector**				
1.	Food processing	Banana chips Banana cue Cassava cake	Micro	K, L, M	30
2.	Furniture making	Bamboo sala sets Bamboo chairs	Micro	A, B, C, D, E, F	6
3.	Rice milling	Milled rice Rice bran	Small	A, B, C	3
4.	Integrated coconut processing	Coconut oil Coco coir Coco charcoal Geotextile Coco vinegar Cocopeat	Medium	Poblacion	1

* The Department of Trade & Industry categorizes enterprises into three, as follows:

Micro	=	enterprises with capitalization up to P 3 million.
Small	=	enterprises with capitalization of more than P 3 million up to P 15 million.
Medium	=	enterprises with capitalization of more than P 15 million up to P 100 million.
Large	=	those capitalized above Php100 million.

	Feasible Opportunity	Target Product or Service	Enterprise Category*	Location (Barangay)	No. of Enterprise
C.	**Services Sector**				
1.	Computer shop	Computer assembly Computer repairs Encoding & printing	Micro	Poblacion	3
2.	Beauty shop	Haircut Manicure Pedicure Makeup	Micro	Poblacion	5
3.	Water supply system (Level 3)	Portable water	Small	Murok-burok	1
D.	**Tourism Sector**				
1.	Eco-tourism	Guided tours Souvenir items	Small	Panayuran	1
2.	Beach resort	Cottages for rent Entertainment	Small	G, H, I, J	4

Part 2 The Municipal Enterprise Development Plan

This part presents the Municipal Enterprise Development Plan in the context of the information discussed in Part 1. The last six chapters of the plan report fall within this part.

Chapter 3 Enterprise Development Framework

Municipal Vision

Simply reproduce in this subsection the municipal vision statement crafted through Workshop #3 (refer to Chapter 9).

Municipal Mission

Also reproduce the municipal mission statement here that was crafted through Workshop #4 (refer to Chapter 9).

Objectives

We emphasize that *development objectives* are positive *milestones* achieved in the course of implementing a person's or an organization's mission. Such is why we said, in Chapter 6, that a good mission statement is one that provides the framework for developing objectives and strategy, for defining critical success factors, and for making resource allocation choices.

Objectives are set around certain key result areas or KRAs. The latter should be easy enough to read from a well crafted mission statement. The KRAs reflect the core values of the LGU leadership, employees, and the LGU constituencies in general. To illustrate our point, let us revisit the mission statement of the Municipality of Calbiga, Samar reproduced below. What KRAs are apparent in this mission statement?

**Mission Statement of the
Municipality of Calbiga, Samar**

The Municipal Government of Calbiga is committed to:

Create local employment and income opportunities in close partnership with the private sector;

Formulate local policies supportive of the development of the micro, cottage and small enterprises (MCSEs) sector as well as the ecotourism sector;

Improve local capacities in sustainable utilization and management of natural resources, thereby securing the survival of the present and future generations of Calbiganons; and

> *Develop a professional and happy core of civil servants with a deep sense of public service."*

From the first sentence, there is *employment and income*; from the second, *support policies formulation*; from the third, *local capacity-building*; and from the fourth, *LGU staff development*. Of course, there are far more KRAs to address, depending upon the vision and the mission statements. For instance, you have agricultural productivity, land tenure, local revenues, environmental rehabilitation and protection, rural accessibility, and the like.

Meanwhile, a way to present the objectives around these KRAs is through a matrix shown Exh. 30. Adapted from the widely popular logical framework or logframe pioneered by the USAID, this four-by-four format shows the KRAs on the first column; the corresponding objectively verifiable indicators on the second column; the means of verification on the third; and the assumptions on the fourth and last column. The latter (i.e., assumptions) are factors or conditions external to the LGU but factors or conditions must occur, nonetheless, if the objectives must be met.

Logframe gurus advise that an objective is simply a positive statement of a negative condition. Thus, the objective for a condition of low or inadequate local capacities would be *improved capacities*; degraded coastal resources may be stated as *rehabilitated coastal resources*; and low household incomes as *increased household incomes*.

Exhibit 30

Sample Statements of Development Objectives

KEY RESULT AREA OBJECTIVE	OBJECTIVELY VERIFIABLE INDICATOR	MEANS OF VERIFICATION	ASSUMPTION
1) Employment			
Increased employment opportunities for local people.	300 local people are employed each year beginning in 2003.	Records of the Business Permit Office.	Necessary local skills required by employers are present.
2) Household incomes			
Increased household incomes	20% increase in average farm household income beginning in 2006.	Sample surveys of farm families	Farm households adopt the technologies recommended.
3) Environmental rehabilitation and protection			
Rehabilitated and protected coastal and forestry resources.	30 hectares of mangrove area are planted to bakhaw by end of 2005.	Ocular inspection.	Funds are available for the purpose.
Improved enforcement of forestry and fisheries laws	Decreased incidence of illegal fishing and illegal logging activities beginning in 2006.	Police blotter. Periodic community consultations.	The affected upland farmers and fisherfolk cooperate with law enforcement authorities.
4) Capacity Building			
Improved capacities of upland farmers in the application of technologies appropriate to upland condition.	30 farms each year are able to apply SALT beginning in 2003.	Monitoring reports of agricultural technicians. Ocular inspection.	Farmers have access to credit.
Improved capacities of fisherfolk in managing coastal resources.	10 hectares of denuded mangroves are reforested each year beginning in 2005.	Monitoring reports of agricultural technicians. Ocular inspection.	Satisfactory tenurial arrangement is awarded to fisherfolk.
5) LGU Staff Development			
Improved knowledge, skills and attitudes of LGU Staff.	Key LGU employees shall have undergone trainings relevant to their jobs by end of 2005.	Training reports.	No reduction on

Chapter 4 Strategic Options

This chapter presents the strategic choices of the LGU. These choices refer to enterprises or products in which the locality enjoys some competitive advantages in such areas as resource base, technology, and markets, among others. This chapter, therefore, necessarily presents the products or enterprise choices made by each sector in the barangay during the process we call *value analysis*.

In addition, other enterprises or products that the planning team consider critical to a rational and sustainable development of a specific economic sector or sub-sector are also presented here.

For example, to effectively promote and develop the livestock and poultry subsector, it may be wise to establish a mini feedmill as an *anchor enterprise*. This would supply the basic animal feeds and supplements required by the local animal and poultry raisers.

Similarly, to effectively raise rice production, it may be wise to invest in a certified seeds production enterprise to respond to the requirements of the rice farmers for high yielding seed varieties.

There are alternative strategic options that the municipality can choose from. These include: (1) status quo; (2) vertical expansion; (3) horizontal expansion; (4) diversification; and (5) divestment.

Meanwhile, by *status quo*, we mean either no change in products already being produced, or no change in geographic markets to which the products of the locality have been traditionally moved.

By *vertical expansion*, we mean expanding the market for an existing product within an existing geographic market, or expanding the production of an existing commodity for an existing and/or new geographic markets.

By *horizontal expansion*, we mean penetrating other geographic market or markets for an existing product.

By *diversification*, we mean either the production of new commodities for an existing market, or the penetration of new market segments (e.g., hotels, students) within an existing market for an existing product.

Finally, by *divestment*, we mean either a shift from an existing product to a new one, or withdrawal of an existing product from an existing market in favor of another, or withdrawal of the product altogether from an existing market.

The product-market matrix shown on Exhibit 31-34 illustrates the various options that the LGU can choose from.

Exhibit 31
Strategic Option: Status Quo

PRODUCT / MARKET	EXISTING MARKET	NEW MARKET
Copra	Tacloban City	

Exhibit 3 2
Strategic Option: Market Extension
(From local traders to exporters)

PRODUCT / MARKET	EXISTING MARKET	NEW MARKET
Copra	Local copra traders	Exporters

Exhibit 33

Strategic Option: Product Diversification

(Diversify from copra to virgin oil and coir fiber)

PRODUCT / MARKET	EXISTING MARKET	NEW MARKET
Copra	Local copra traders	Oil millers
Virgin oil		Mercury Drug
Coir fiber		Fiber exporters

Exhibit 34

Strategic Option: Divestment

(Shift from copra to virgin oil)

PRODUCT / MARKET	EXISTING MARKET	POTENTIAL MARKET
Virgin oil	Mercury Drug	

Describe the strategic options, by economic sector (i.e., Agriculture & Fisheries; Trade & Industry; Services; Tourism). It is wise to present the strategic options, by specific time zone (i.e., immediate term; short term; medium term; long term). The following are examples:

Agriculture & Fisheries Sector

Immediate Term Options (less than 1 year)
> Expand the production of mussel for the Leyte-Samar market.

> Expand the mussel market to cover the households in the cities of Cebu, Mandaue and Lapu-lapu.

Short Term Options (1-2 Yrs.)
> Diversify production of marine commodities to include mudcrab and *lapu-lapu* (in pens) for the existing markets.

Diversify crop production under coconut to cover such fruits and vegetables as pineapple, *mungo* and *amargoso* for the existing provincial market.

Medium Term Option (3-5 years)

Diversify marine production to cover dried seaweed for the export market.

Long Term Options (6 years and beyond)

Expand the market for *lapu-lapu* to respond to the export demand from China.

Diversify fisheries production to include cultured *bangus* for the local markets.

Trade & Industry Sector

Immediate Term Options

Expand the production of handicrafts for existing and new markets.

Expand the rice milling capacity to respond to local productivity improvements and increases in irrigated area.

Short Term Option

Diversify the production of handicrafts for existing and new markets to cover such products as placemats, handbags and coin purses.

Medium Term Options

Diversify processing activities to include processing of boneless *bangus*, canned *bangus* and canned mussel products for the domestic markets.

Expand the market for handicrafts to cover the export market.

Long Term Option
Diversify the market for processed *bangus* and mussel products to cover the export markets.

Services Sector

Immediate Term Option
Expand the market for water system to cover households in nearby barangays along the Maharlika highway.

Short Term Option
Diversify into such services as computer assembly and computer maintenance for the local market.

Medium Term Options (3-5 Yrs.)
Diversify into technical and vocational education for the local market.

Diversify into eco-tourism to capture the provincial and regional markets.

Long Term Option
Expand the market for eco-tourism to cover foreign tourists.

Chapter 5 Strategic Interventions

This chapter presents the strategic interventions envisioned to effectively exploit the strategic options open to the LGU. Strategic interventions refer to the key factors that must be in place so that the strategic options can materialize, in effect attaining the LGU's development objectives, accomplishing its mission and, eventually, contributing to the realization of its vision.

What these key factors are will depend upon the *gaps* that have to be bridged so that the strategic options can come to reality. These factors will necessarily vary from place to place because of differences in geographic needs or requirements for development.

In any case, these key interventions are lifted from the Barangay Enterprise Development Plans formulated by sectoral participants in the Barangay Strategic Planning Workshops. The Municipal Planning Team, though, is expected to propose additional interventions as necessary.

The following interventions are commonly required:

Credit Assistance Program

Describe the program by presenting its objective(s); the credit or financing scheme; interest rate; borrowing criteria; sources of credit funds (e.g., development fund of LGU, credit line with existing development banks, credit cooperatives, guarantee funds, etc.); and estimates of credit requirements, by enterprise and economic sector. The latter information can be derived simply by multiplying the number of enterprises proposed by ballpark estimates of the start-up capital requirements of the enterprise. In this, the planner can be guided by the enterprise categorization of the Department of Trade and Industry (DTI), as follows:

Micro enterprises are those with capitalization of up to P 3 million;
Small enterprises are those with capitalization of up to P 15 million;
Medium enterprises are those capitalized up to P 100 million; and
Large enterprises are those capitalized above P 100 million.
Present the estimated cost of credit requirements in a statistical table (see Exhibit 35 for sample).

Exhibit 35
Estimated Credit Requirements ('000 P)

ENTERPRISE	REFERENCE	CREDIT REQUIREMENTS
A. Agriculture & Fisheries		
1. Palay production	10 enterprises x P 10,000	100
2. Cattle production	20 enterprises x P 35,000	700
Sub-Total		800
B. Trade & Industry		
1. Mat-weaving	30 enterprises x P 5,000	150
2. Integrated coconut processing	1 enterprise x P 30 million	30,000
Sub-Total		30,000
C. Services		
1. Computer shop	3 enterprises x P 150,000	450
Sub-Total		450
D. Tourism		
1. Beach resort	2 enterprises x P 1 million	2,000
Sub-Total		2,000
TOTAL		**33,250**

Infrastructure Support Program

Describe the program by presenting its objective(s); the specific infrastructure facilities needed, by specific location and size (e.g., 180 linear meters of bridges; 20 km. of barangay roads; 30,000 m2 enterprise park; 0.5 hectare bus and jeepney terminal; etc.); and ballpark estimates of the cost of infrastructures that the municipal engineer should be able to provide (see Exh. 36 for sample cost estimates).

Exhibit 36

Estimated Cost of Infrastructure Program ('000 P)

	ROAD LINK	REFERENCE	COST
1.	Barangay A to Poblacion (new construction)	10 kms x P 3 million/km	30,000
2.	Barangay B to C (rehab)	5 km x P 1.5 million/km	7,500
	TOTAL		**37,500**

Capacity Building Program

Describe the program by presenting its overall objective(s); proposed training modules; module objectives; target participants and their number; training content; training methodology (e.g., study tours; cross visits; lecture/ discussion; workshops; case studies; etc.); targeted training suppliers; and ballpark estimates of training cost.

Present the cost estimates in a statistical table (see Exh. 37 for sample).

Exhibit 37

Estimated Cost of Capacity-Building Program ('000 P)

	NATURE OF TRAINING	REFERENCE	COST
A.	**LGU Staff**		
	1. Investment promotions	5 participants (pax) x P 10,000/pax	50
	2. Coastal resource management	10 pax x P 10,000/pax	100
	3. Study tours	2 tours x 5 pax/tour x P 10,000/pax	100
	Sub-Total		250
B.	**Cooperatives**		
	1. Business management	10 coops x 3 pax/coop x P 500/pax/day x 3 days	45
	2. Simplified accounting & bookkeeping	10 coops x 3 pax/coop x P 500/pax/day x 3 days	45
	3. Credit collections & management	10 coops x 3 pax/coop x P 500/pax/day x 3 days	45
	Sub-Total		135
C.	**Individual Entrepreneurs**		

1. Business awareness seminar	200 pax x P 500/pax	100
2. Seaweed farming	300 pax x x P 500/pax/ day x 2 days	300
3. Coir fiber production	20 pax x P 500/pax/day x 2 days	20
	Sub-Total	420
	TOTAL	**805**

Marketing Assistance

Marketing is one aspect of business in which most micro and small enterprises are disadvantaged. The most common marketing problems include unfavorable prices offered by the traders, inability to penetrate bigger markets and lack of reliable and timely marketing information with which to make more rational production and marketing decisions. In this regard, marketing assistance becomes a key intervention that the LGU may be able to provide.

Describe your proposed marketing assistance. This may come in such forms as:

Provision of reliable and timely marketing information on prices in alternative markets using such media as printed price bulletin or using community bulletin boards through which market prices and announcements on products with ready buyers can be made.

Preparation, reproduction and distribution of directory of alternative product buyers in major trading centers.

Linkage with the DTI such that the local producers may avail of the opportunity to sell their products during the trade fairs organized by the DTI.

Describe how marketing information may be generated. In this regard, the Bureau of Agricultural Statistics, the statistical and economic intelligence arm of the Department of Agriculture, is a good source of information on domestic and export prices of agricultural and fishery products. Similarly, the DTI is a good source of information on prices, and supply and demand data on agro-industrial products.

Finally, describe the organizational arrangements and the necessary manpower that would be tasked to implement this intervention, and provide ballpark estimates of the cost associated with this key Intervention. Present the cost estimates in a statistical table (see Exh. 38 for sample).

Exhibit 38
Estimated Cost of Marketing Assistance Program ('000 P)

	ITEM	REFERENCE	COST
1.	Production of buyers' directory	2000 copies x P 30/copy	60
2.	Price bulletins	10 bulletins x P 2,500	25
3.	Municipal website development	Lump sum	25
	TOTAL		110

Environmental Management Program

In the face of global degradation of the environment, environmental management has become an imperative intervention for all nations and governments today. For unless the continuing degradation of the environment is arrested, sustainable development cannot happen, in effect jeopardizing the material survival of the present and future generations— not only of human beings, but also of plants, animals and other life forms that depend on the resources of nature for survival.

An environmental management plan is normally contained in the land use plan of the municipality. If the latter plan exists and has been updated, simply insert it in this chapter. If not, then the Municipal Planning Team will have to draft the environmental management plan, which focuses on three components. These are singled out and discussed in the following sections.

Watershed Management

Watershed refers to such natural resources as the uplands, forests, wildlife, and water systems such as rivers, lakes, streams, creeks and coastal waters. Accordingly, watershed management means the management of these natural resources with a view to prevent environmental degradation and promote the sustainable use of these resources.

Describe your watershed management plan. The latter should be based on existing realities or conditions of the watershed areas, the reasons behind these, and their apparent adverse effects on the productivity of agricultural lands, river system and the coastal waters.

The plan should be able to identify the most critical resources (e.g., uplands, forests, river system), spell out measurable objectives and draw up corresponding strategies (in terms of projects and programs), including policies, to attain the objectives.

Describe the recommended institutional arrangements for watershed management and monitoring, and provide estimates of the costs involved.

Coastal Resource Management

Coastal resource management refers to the management of such coastal resources as the coastal waters, mangrove forests, sea grasses, corral reefs and the various marine lives such that these resources can support the material survival of the present and future generations.

Describe the coastal resource management plan in terms of its focal resources, its measurable objectives, its strategies and policies, and the institutional arrangements with respect to plan implementation and monitoring. Non-coastal municipalities, of course, would have none of this plan.

Pollution Control

Finally, pollution control deals with the management of wastes from domestic, industrial and other sources to prevent the pollution of land, air and the fresh and seawater environment.

Describe your pollution control plan in terms of its focal areas, its measurable objectives, its strategies (in terms of projects and programs), support policies and institutional arrangements for plan implementation and monitoring.

Other Strategic Interventions

There could be a lot more to the strategic interventions singled out above. Other LGUs, for instance, may see the need for the delivery of business advisory services as a way to raise the chances of local enterprises, especially those belonging to the micro, cottage and small enterprise categories, for survival, stability and growth.

In any case, the appropriate interventions would necessarily depend upon a good reading of the *gaps* that stand in the way of the development of the various economic sectors of the local economy. Of course, the financial capability of the LGU would necessarily shape the types of intervention it can provide.

Provide estimates of cost involved in the implementation off the environmental management program (see Exh. 39 for sample).

Exhibit 39

Estimated Cost of Environmental Management Program ('000 P)

ITEM	REFERENCE	COST
A. Watershed management 1. Upland reforestation project	10 hectares x P 15,000/hectare	150
Sub-Total		150
B. Coastal resource management		
1. Mangrove reforestation	100 ha x P 18,000/ha	1,800
Sub-Total		1,800
C. Pollution control		
1. Consultancy to design zero waste management system	30 persondays x P 5,000/personday	150
2. Capital cost for zero waste management system	Lumpsum	5,000
Sub-Total		5,150
TOTAL		7,100

Chapter 6 Plan Implementation Arrangements

This chapter presents the mechanism recommended to implement your MEDP. The chapter may be divided into the following sections.

Chief Implementation Unit

Normally, it is the Municipal Planning and Development Office (MPDO) that is tasked to anchor the implementation of the MEDP. In most cases, however, the MPDO is manned by only one person who may also double as civil registrar or as concurrent head of the business permit unit of the LGU. Under this circumstance, it may be wise to create an inter-unit committee to oversee the implementation of the plan. This committee may be comprised by the Municipal Planning and Development Coordinator as chair; and the Municipal Engineer, Municipal Agriculturist, Municipal Treasurer, Municipal Social Welfare and Development Officer, and the Municipal Budget Officer as members.

Plan Implementation Schedule

Show the plan implementation schedule in a Gantt Chart (see Exhibit 40 for sample format). Implementation is usually done in phases, which may include the following:

Pre-Implementation Phase

Activities In this phase would cover the following:

> Preparation for the presentation of the plan before the Sangguniang Bayan (SB) for comments, revision or approval;
> Revision of the plan (in case of SB comments);
> Presentation of revised plan to the SB for approval; and
> Reproduction of approved MEDP.

Investment Promotion Phase

This phase aims at promoting the investments identified in the plan to prospective local investors for purposes of generating investment interests from prospective investors and donors.

The latter would include individual entrepreneurs, partnerships, corporations or cooperatives, including such agencies as the provincial government, DPWH and bilateral or multi-lateral financing organizations.

Activities associated with this phase may include:

> Preparation of investment promotion materials (e.g., brochure, leaflets, etc.) including project feasibility studies;
> Organization of and preparation for the holding of local investors' forum;
> Conduct of investors' forum;

Consultations and negotiations with formal credit suppliers (e.g., local banks; credit cooperatives; investment houses) for possible financing arrangements for local investors with financing needs; and Consultations and negotiations with provincial government and DPWH for possible for infrastructure projects.

Investment promotion is a continuing activity and is expected to generate investment decisions.

Plan Implementation Phase

Activities in this phase may include:

Preparation of detailed engineering plans for support infrastructure projects;

Formulation and passage of municipal policies or ordinances in support of enterprise promotion and development; and

Implementation and monitoring of support infrastructure projects.

Exhibit 40
Gantt Chart of Activities, Year 1-5

ACTIVITY	TIME FRAME						RESPONSIBILITY
	Y_1				Y_2	Y_{3-5}	
	Q1	Q2	Q3	Q4			
A. Pre-implementation Phase							
1							
2							
3							
4							
B. Investment Promotions Phase							
1							
2							
3							
4							
5							

C. Plan Implementation Phase
1
2
3
D. Monitoring & Evaluation

Administrative and Operating Budget

This final section provides cost estimates relative to the implementation of the plan. Present the budget in a table as in the following sample.

Exhibit 41

Administrative and Operating Budget ('000 P)

ITEM	REFERENCE	BUDGET
Plan reproduction	500 copies x P 50/copy	25.00
Design and reproduction of investment promotion materials (brochure)	1,000 copies x P 10/copy	10.00
Conduct of investors forum	100 participants x P 100/pax	10.00
Meetings with funding agencies	1 meeting per quarter x 12 quarters P 1,500/meeting	18.00
Preparation of feasibility studies	4 studies x P 150,000/study	600.00
Communications	P 2,000/month x 36 months	72.00
Transport/travel	1 round trip/quarter/officer x 12 quarters x 2 officers x P 10,000/RT	240.00
Representation allowance	P 5,000/month x 36 months	180.00
Office supplies & materials	P 3,000/month x 36 months	108.00
TOTAL		**1263.00**

Chapter 7 Financing Requirements and Financing Plan

Total Investment Requirements

This section presents estimates of the total investment requirements of the plan. The major investment areas are, of course, the *strategic interventions*, including the administrative and operating costs associated with managing the implementation of the plan. Present the total investment requirements of the plan in a statistical table. A sample format is presented in Exhibit 42.

Exhibit 42

Estimated Investment Requirements ('000 P)

ITEM	REFERENCE	COST
A. Credit Support Program	Exhibit 35	
Sub-Total		
B. Infrastructure Support Program	Exhibit 36	
Sub-Total		
C. Capacity-Building Program	Exhibit 37	
Sub-Total		
D. Marketing Assistance Program	Exhibit 38	
Sub-Total		
E. Environmental Management Program	Exhibit 39	
Sub-Total		
F. Administrative & Operating Cost	Exhibit 41	
Total		
Contingencies 10%		
GRAND TOTAL		

Financing Plan

This section presents the LGU's proposal as to how the investments identified in the plan shall be funded. A sample financing plan format, with Exhibit 42 as reference, is shown on Exhibit 43.

Exhibit 43
Financing Plan

	ITEM	TOTAL COST	LGU	BENEFICIARIES	DONORS	OTHERS
A.	Credit support program					
B.	Infrastructure support program					
C.	Capacity-building program					
D.	Marketing assistance program					
E.	Environmental management program					
F.	Administrative & operating cost					
G.	Contingencies					
	Total					
	GRAND TOTAL					
	Ratio (%)					

Chapter 8 Plan Monitoring and Evaluation

This final chapter presents the system for plan implementation monitoring and evaluation. The system should be able to address such basic questions as: What to monitor? When to monitor? How to monitor? And who will monitor? The chapter may be developed according to the following sections.

Monitoring and Evaluation System

Formulating a logical framework or logframe will make it easier to monitor and evaluate the progress of plan implementation. A complete logframe (presented in a planning matrix) consists of four (4) sequential columns: (1) Narrative Summary; (2) Objectively Verifiable Indicator or OVI; (3) Means of Verification or MOV; and (4) Assumption.

The first column has 5 components: (1) Goal or Goals which are long-term results expected of an intervention; (2) Purpose or Purposes which refer to the changes the intervention is expected to make in order to attain the Goal/s; (3) the Outputs or milestones that the intervention is expected to put in place in order to achieve the Purpose/s; (4) the key Activities that have to be accomplished in order to produce the Outputs or milestones; and (5) the Inputs (budget and manpower) that have to be provided in order to carry out the key Activities. The OVI or OVIs are formulated for each component, including the corresponding MOV or MOVs, and the Assumption or Assumptions. The latter are external factors or conditions over which the intervention or project has no control but which have to be present if the goal/s must be attained, the purpose/s achieved, the outputs or milestones put in place, and the activities carried out.

Exhibit 44 below is presented as a sample logframe or planning matrix.

Exhibit 44
Planning Matrix

NARRATIVE SUMMARY	OBJECTIVELY VERIFIABLE INDICATOR	MEANS OF VERIFICATION	ASSUMPTION
Goal:			
Improved palay farm household incomes	Average annual household income rises 30% by the end of 2016.	Sample household income & expenditure surveys	Farmers adopt recommended technologies.
Purpose:			
Increased average yield of palay	By end of 2014, average palay yield has risen from 3 tons to 6 tons per hectare.	Focus group discussions with participating farmers	Farmers adopt the technology package recommended.
Outputs:			
Necessary farm inputs are provided.	Certified seeds are made available to 100 participating farmers beginning in 2013.	Records of the Municipal Agriculturist Office	Funds are made available

NARRATIVE SUMMARY	OBJECTIVELY VERIFIABLE INDICATOR	MEANS OF VERIFICATION	ASSUMPTION
Communal Irrigation is rehabilitated.	100 ha of palay farms are served by communal irrigation beginning in 2013.	Records of the Office of the Municipal Agriculturist	External funds are available for communal irrigation.
Activities:			
Conduct farmers' applied training in recommended palay production technology.	By end of 2013, 100 farmers have attended applied training in recommended palay production technology.	Records of the Office of the Municipal Agriculturist (OMA)	There is demand for training from farmers.
Rehabilitate communal irrigation system.	Rehab of existing communal irrigation system is completed by end of 2013.	Ocular inspection	Rehab funds are provided by National Irrigation Administration (NIA).
	100 hectares of palay farms are served by irrigation beginning in 2014.	Records of the NIA and OMA.	

The foregoing matrix depicts an overall plan and generally a longer time period. In practice, this has to be reduced into shorter periods, preferably into annual plans, broken down into quarterly targets. For this, the same planning matrix can be used. By the end of each quarter, the monitoring and evaluation team can sit down to assess the progress of plan implementation, and to re-plan, if necessary.

Monitoring and Evaluation Team

The plan implementation structure proposed in Chapter 6 is expected to provide for a plan monitoring and evaluation team. Ideally, this team should be external to the plan implementers for purposes of objectivity. But, in practice, those involved in plan implementation also perform the monitoring and evaluation tasks.

Appendices

It is advisable to put the Barangay Enterprise Development Plans in the appendix, including other pieces of information about the municipality not presented in the MEDP report.

References

Gaon, Benjamin V. and Villacorta Carmelo R. *A National Manual on Planning, Implementation, Monitoring, and Evaluation of Integrated Rural Development (IRD) Projects*: (CIRDAP/NACIAD: September, 1986).

Go, Josiah. *Contemporary Marketing Strategy in the Philippine Setting.* (Philippines: May, 1992)

Kindleberger, Charles P. *Economic Development.* 2nd Edition (Tokyo: McGraw-Hill Book Company, Inc., 1965)

Kotler, Philip. *Marketing Management: Analysis, Planning, Implementation and Control.* 6th Edition (Evanston, Illinois: Northwestern University Press, 1988)

Scott, Cynthia D. et al. *Organizational Vision, Values and Mission.* (Menlo Park, California: Crisp Publications, Inc., 1993)